PRAISE FOR *MASTERING THE GAME*

This book is a great guide for those who are master gamers at home and wish to be as influential and competent at work. You'll be amazed at how much you already know and how easy it will be to transfer critical business skills after reading *Mastering The Game.* At the same time, hiring managers and organizational leaders will find keen insight on the workforce of today and tomorrow!

Marshall Goldsmith author of the New York Times and global bestseller *What Got You Here Won't Get You There*

Often times, the answers to our greatest challenges are hidden in plain sight. Jon Harrison presents an inspired look at how the most valued traits in business are already being practiced while playing video games – and makes thought provoking illustrations for how to draw out these ideas in the workplace. This book may hold the key to unlocking the significant potential of the next generation of leaders.

Mark Panciera, *President of The Pacific Institute, US Operations*

Jon has put into words what gamers have been telling their parents for years: videogames are *good* for you. He lays out how the skills & ideas our favorite videogames intrinsically teach us -- overcoming obstacles, maximizing your strengths, and triumphing over your fears -- can directly apply to your happiness and success.

Chris Hatala, *Final Boss, Games Done Legit entertainment*

In *Mastering The Game*, Jon Harrison shares his vision for how video games can be used to teach business and life lessons. Professionals and gamers alike will benefit from reading and applying these ideas.

Kimanzi Constable, Author of the Publishers Weekly best-selling book, *Are You Living or Existing? 9 Steps to Change Your Life*

Video games can teach us lessons in real life. Jon Harrison is one of the best at showing us how. Read his book.

Patrick Stafford, *Professional Writer and Journalist, pdstafford.com*

MASTERING THE GAME

MASTERING THE GAME

WHAT VIDEO GAMES CAN TEACH US ABOUT SUCCESS IN LIFE

COPYRIGHT

DEDICATION

This book is dedicated to my wife Carmen and my son Dante

Your love and support mean the world to me.

I am so proud of who you are.

ACKNOWLEDGEMENT

To Mark Panciera, Tor Constantino, Joel Caprio, Ray Johnson, Jared Easley, Mike Kim, Kimanzi Constable, Shawn Smith, Johnny Lee Philips, Jody Maberry, Dr. Ryan Gray, Ellory Wells, Ryan Arnold, Bruce Hurley, and my parents, Joe and Pat Harrison – thank you for your support and encouragement in pursuit of my crazy ideas.

TABLE OF CONTENTS

Foreword... 8

Introduction... 13

Part I: Video Games and Learning

    Pressing Start... 20

    Allegamy In Practice 32

    Not Quite Gamification 55

Part II: Transferable Skills

    Connecting The Dots................................... 65

    Strategic Planning...................................... 81

    Adaptability 94

    Change Management 105

    Clearing The Entitlement Level................... 127

    Personal Accountability............................. 138

    Innovation... 155

    Strengths 166

    Learning.. 175

    Communication & Listening........................ 186

    Teambuilding & Collaboration.................... 204

    Knowledge Sharing................................... 231

    Persistence & Grit 239

Conclusion.. 251

Epilogue... 263

Bonus Chapter.. 266

FOREWORD

Emerson, NJ. 1987. I remember it vividly. My parents bought me my first video game system, the Nintendo Entertainment System Deluxe Set. It was everything a nine-year old boy could want; a gun, a robot called R.O.B., games like *Duck Hunt* and the all-time classic, *Super Mario Bros.*

My love for videogames was born.

Unfortunately, so was my need for corrective eyewear. I played so much that I had to get glasses in the 5th grade. Furious, my parents threw away my Nintendo just a few months later. For the rest of my adolescent and teen years, videogames were forbidden in our home.

But hey, that's what friends were for.

While Mom and Dad were glad to blame videogames for my ailing vision and faltering grades, I continued my secret obsession with them. My friends and I would play for hours after school (at their house, of course). We'd walk miles just to go to an arcade. You wouldn't believe the storms we braved, the overpasses we crossed, the incredible danger we put ourselves in riding our bicycles down Route 4 in New Jersey just to play *Street Fighter 2*. It was insanity.

But if you asked me at the time, "Why do you love videogames?" I would have thought you were the one that was insane. What kid doesn't like videogames?

As an adult (at least according to age), I can now look back and see how integral videogames were to my development. I can also understand my parents' aversion to them. But like most things that impact us in life, videogames were not a black-or-white issue. They were not completely good (I admit wasting a lot of time playing them). But they weren't completely bad, either.

I'm thankful Jon Harrison has written this book. It details the lessons, skills, and developmental processes I experienced through videogames, and does so in a way I could never articulate. This is important, not just for me as an individual, but also for you and I as members of the human race.

Does this sound like a stretch? Consider that as an 80's kid, I've lived through what many consider to be the most rapid phase of technological advancement in human history. I started my love affair with videogames playing *Super Mario Bros.* on my Nintendo. Just the other day I connected to a server that allows hundreds of thousands of human beings to initiate hundreds of different sessions simultaneously…

…to shoot each other in *Call of Duty: Advanced Warfare*.

9

Twenty years separate these two games, and yes, twenty years is but a drop in the bucket in the whole of human history. Yet in this short time, an entire generation of human beings has had their psychological, physiological, intellectual, auditory, visual, and sensory faculties permanently shaped by videogames, or some derivative thereof. The military now uses them in training simulations. Teachers use them in classrooms to help students with learning disabilities. Kids have built entire cities inside *Minecraft.* Even President Frank Underwood from *House of Cards* plays them to unwind, fictional character notwithstanding. Videogames are but a drop in the bucket, but that drop has resulted in ripples and waves that have forever altered humanity.

Every gamer's experience varies – even within the finite framework of the same game. The same can be said of our individual experiences of movies, or books, or music, or poetry. Yet those mediums have historically been held in higher esteem than videogames.

To that I say this: it doesn't matter if you are a "gamer" or not. It doesn't matter if you think they are stupid, childish, or a waste of time. It doesn't even matter if you think this book is a half-baked attempt at legitimizing videogames as a form of art or entertainment.

What matters is that you likely know someone who plays videogames. What matters is there are millions more that also play them. What really matters – on an intellectual, sociological, *deeper* level – is that we seriously consider the impact videogames have had on us.

Until now, we have not done well in taking stock of this incredibly epic (and incredibly fast) phenomenon. This book moves us in the right direction. Take stock of what Jon shares. You'll discover you have a lot more to offer the world, in part because videogames have given you more than you realized.

Mike Kim

Marketer, businessman, gamer

mikekim.com

MASTERING THE GAME

INTRODUCTION

"This is it. This... is your story. It all begins here."

Auron, Final Fantasy X

"If you do nothing, you will lose nothing. A craven way to live… If you can really call that life. I, for one, cannot."

Aya Brea, Parasite Eve II

Video games. Success.

Leadership. Nintendo.

Productivity. Xbox.

World of Warcraft. Doing something with your life.

For many, these words are at odds. They seem to be antonyms, on the far opposite ends of the scale. But what if I told you that video games contain many secrets to success, productivity, time management, and ways to make a difference in the real world?

I believe they do.

It was early 2014, and I was sitting at my dining room table thinking about what I can offer the world. On the one hand, I have experienced success in my professional life: I have the "manager" title and I am working a well-respected position with an employer I enjoy. The past 7 years of work are with the same employer, almost enough for a gold watch by today's standards. The job is mostly predictable, Monday through Friday, regular business hours. My role is making a positive impact in the world: I help healthcare professionals be more successful in their work.

In addition to my day job, I was writing a blog on the topic of life and leadership lessons, but let's be honest, leadership and productivity blogs are a dime a dozen, maybe even less. I was feeling lost in the mix. I didn't want to keep doing what everyone else was doing, sharing the same books and telling the same stories. We don't need another 50 summaries of the same leadership and management books. We have Amazon for that.

So then I took time to reflect on my hobbies. Sure, I have dabbled in quite a few over the years, but one hobby has stayed with me for almost 30 years: video games. Now for as many leadership blogs that are out there, I wager video game blogs far outnumber personal development and productivity websites. As much as I have been keeping up with my gaming hobby, I am sure I know far less than many of these top-notch gaming bloggers, if for no other reason than my plate is full with a wife, a son, and a demanding full time job. While I am sure many of them are in the same position, I was not ready to jump into that pool just yet. My passion lies elsewhere.

There is a long standing stereotype around video games and video game players: people who play video games "don't have a life." The imagery of young men who are unwilling to grow up and are incapable of succeeding in real life. The individual who has moved back in with their parents, and live in the basement huddled around the light of the TV or computer screen. Yet here I am. I don't fit the stereotype. Quite the opposite. In fact, many of my friends are gamers as well, and they don't fit the stereotype either. Many are successful professionals, even in leadership roles.

I would say that many of the traits that made them successful while playing video games also contributed to their success in the professional world. Then it hit me. Could it be possible that life and leadership lessons could be taught from video games? Can those success traits and principles transfer?

Once reaching "adulthood" many video game enthusiasts deal with criticism of our game playing. As a child, we were challenged to justify what appeared to be a waste of time to many, including our parents and other adults we looked up to. Often, the best defense we can muster is "it improves hand and eye coordination," or as we advanced to playing first person shooters like *Doom* and *Halo* we could claim improved "spatial reasoning." Even the best answers in defense of video games sound like excerpts from a "Things I learned in Kindergarten" poster. "Play nice with others," "learn to share," and "take a nap every day" are examples of the choice wisdom offered. But these ideas don't go far enough.

I believe real depth exists in the expanse of video game mythology, and that ideas and concepts we learn while playing video games can then be translated into the real world around us: into our professional lives, our parenting, and even our relationships. I know this because I believe the concepts found in many video games are based on principles. Principles are ideas that are timeless and remain true, independent of context, culture or even an era. Principles have value and transferability.

Now these principles have a universal appeal to them, and a game that includes these principles has as much truth as a book, a movie, or even a college class containing the same principles. A simple example is the concept of cause-and-effect. Where can you find a more perfect example of feedback than in video games? The game player sends input through a controller, and then action takes place on the screen that is directly related to the input the player has indicated, almost instantaneously - a very clear example of cause-and-effect.

Video games offer a natural framework for transferring ideas and facts. Author of *Game Frame: Using Games as a Strategy for Success*, Aaron Dignan asserts that video games offer a teaching advantage "…Through a structured and challenging system that makes the process of learning rewarding, enables deep engagement, provides a sense of autonomy, and asks us to be heroes in our own stories."

Increasing the potential of video games being leveraged as a teaching tool are many factors, in particular the acceptance and engagement of individuals of all ages, from all walks of life. The reports show that for 2014, 59% of Americans play video games, with the average age hitting 31. Surprisingly, women over the age of 18 represent a larger population than young men under 18.

Jason Allaire, Ph.D., associate professor of psychology at North Carolina State University and co-director of the Gains Through Gaming Lab comments on this shift in game playing demographics: "People of all ages play video games. There is no longer a 'stereotype game player,' but instead a game player could be your grandparent, your boss, or even your professor."

More than a passing fad or a niche hobby, video games are here to stay and growing in influence. I consider it a responsibility, even an obligation, to embrace and unlock the powerful potential for good that video games represent.

I hope you will join me in this endeavor.

PART I: VIDEO GAMES AND LEARNING

PRESSING START

"The right man in the wrong place can make all the difference in the world."

The G Man, Half Life 2

I have been an avid reader my whole life. While still in elementary school, I remember my parents buying me a collection of the "classic" novels – books like *Treasure Island, Moby Dick,* and *Robinson Crusoe.* I loved the sense of adventure, danger, and excitement, and I would often stay awake late, even after my parents had gone to bed, so I could keep reading. I remember one type of story in particular that was very interesting: the allegory.

Works such as *Pilgrim's Progress,* the *Chronicles of Narnia, Animal Farm, Don Quixote* and *Aesop's Fables* captured my imagination, as I enjoyed trying to find the parallels between the story and the intended representation in reality. I have also found myself drawn to science fiction movies (often based on books) that offer symbolism and analogy in their storytelling narrative. Some of my favorites include: *the Wizard of Oz, Blade Runner, the Lord of the Rings, Fight Club,* and *the Matrix.*

What I find most interesting is this idea that individuals can be taught and even spurred to thinking about things in new ways through storytelling and allegory. Books offer a self-paced experience, where the reader can pause and reflect, revisit and re-read, or even skip around within the story. I am one of those individuals who scribbles notes in the margins of my books, ruining them for future readers, capturing my own ideas as I consume the material. Books can actively engage the imagination, as the writer describes the world and events contained within, but the reader overlays their own interpretation through their mind's eye in a way that creates a unique experience for each reader.

Movies can build on the strengths of the story, and provide another layer of experience through compelling visuals and heighten the experience with a masterful soundtrack. While movies can intensify the experience, the time limitations of the format cause many details to be lost when converting from written works, and remove much of the imagination's engagement for the viewer. When we watch the 2013 film adaptation of *the Great Gatsby*, we are not afforded the opportunity to imagine the physical appearance of Nick Carraway and Jay Gatsby, but instead, we see the faces of Tobey Maguire and Leonardo DiCaprio.

The soundtrack for this movie is also an element under criticism. The decision to include many modern rap songs as part of the soundtrack, jarringly removes the work from the context in which it was depicting and forces it into modern context in a way that reveals the challenge of the passive nature of the medium. Movies remain a popular form of entertainment that provide us with moving experiences, but for the most part remain limited by several of the previously mentioned strengths.

Compared to books and movies, video games offer a great opportunity to combine the advantages of both, within the same media. Storytelling, written word, visuals, audio, self-directed pacing, and active engagement all exists within the media of video games. There is great potential in this area to develop amazing works of art which can also provide instruction and self-paced learning, while prompting and engaging creativity and imagination. Video games have historically been dismissed as a child's game, immature, addictive, or worse yet, the inspiration behind horrific violent acts. To easily dismiss video games in this way is a great mistake and a denial of their true potential.

Valiant efforts have been made to create learning games, or "edutainment," but too often these "games" miss their mark. Early attempts like *Reader Rabbit* and *Mathblaster* were too focused on the learning, neglecting the elements that make video games compelling. The challenge with many educational games is the player starts a game with the expectation that the game is designed to teach. Already it sounds less like fun and more like work.

Yet the opportunity to truly leverage video games as a teaching tool cannot be missed. In many ways, video games are all about teaching. By way of example, consider the following list of names: Roy

Campbell, Jill Valentine, Chris Redfield, Leon S. Kennedy, John Marston, Professor Herschel Layton, Gabriel Belmont, Gordon Freeman, Sam Fisher, Genjuro Kibagami, Ken Masters, Chun Li, Shang Tsung, Sonya Blade, Nathan Drake, Elena Fisher, Cloud Strife, Tifa Lockhart, Dr. Wily, Lara Croft, and Sarah Bryant. This list of individuals are people who I know, and I can provide you with rather specific information about.

They also share one thing in common: everyone listed is a video game character.

I think about all the information stored in my brain which is tied to, or learned from, video games, and the possibilities are staggering. To prove my point, just ask any video game player to list out the name of video game worlds or towns they have visited, describe classes of characters, discuss statistics that are game related, or recite complex combinations of buttons pressed for special moves and combinations in fighting games. The learning mechanism's success is difficult to debate. It is the relevance of the information that is the issue.

What if these towns were real world locations? What if button combinations represented steps in a scientific or mathematical formula? What if the historical events told in the tales of epic quests were actually a re-telling of our own history? Consider all the learning taking place in the over 6 million years of actual history in game play time recorded in just the game *World of Warcraft*. Also consider that so far, I have only mentioned the possibility for rote memorization, not breaching on topics of creativity, systems thinking, or innovation.

Classic Literature: The Game

Beyond the potential mentioned for allegory within gaming, another potential along the journey to realizing the full potential of gaming, is a clever repurposing of existing classical works. I would be quite interested in seeing a developer attempt to re-create or retell a classic literature story in video game form. Not just an adaptation of the subject matter, but a definitive recreation of the book. I have every reason to believe this could be very successful, especially when I look at an existing game that comes pretty close in execution.

Square Enix and Disney teamed up to create an action role-playing game, *Kingdom Hearts*. This game combined original characters, favorites from the *Final Fantasy* franchise, and most notably characters from Disney movies. The stories and game narrative were intertwined with a final result that is very impressive. The game is a standalone work into itself, but what was most notable to me was the environment created around the Disney intellectual property. As you played through various scenarios which included excerpts from famous Disney animated films, you actually took an interactive role within these familiar game worlds.

Various segments of the game felt as if you had stepped directly onto the set of a Disney animated film, and you were taking part in a retelling of Disney movies including *Cinderella, Tron, the Lion King,* and even *the Little Mermaid*. In many cases the original voice actors were used or talent was hired sounding so similar to the original Disney voices that only a hardcore fan would be able to tell the difference.

Since Square Enix and Disney can team up to create a game successfully capturing the true feel of these iconic movies why isn't it reasonable to think a publisher could re-create existing classics such as *Treasure Island,* the *Hound of the Baskervilles* or any other number of literary classics? These games could be a highly interactive and definitive version of the written work, with details and learning opportunities unrivaled by any other media.

Allegamy: Old Meets New

Taking the idea a step further, consider video games engage the user in a multi-sensory experience that can span significant amounts of time. I recall playing *Final Fantasy VII* to the point the in game timer hit 99 hours and 99 minutes and then stopped. That is time I chose to spend, learning, working, and solving the problems of a fictional world. What if all that time, I had been playing a game which was an allegory, or if you will entertain my own terminology, *allegamy*. Imagine a video games designed with a secondary interpretation, revealing a lesson with real world applicability.

An allegamy is not a simulation. When I imagine the possibilities of simulations, the sobering concepts within science fiction works in the vein of *Enders Game* and *War Games,* come to mind. In both works individuals are engaging in what they believe is a video game or simulation, only to learn their activity in the game has real world impact. While simulations have the ability to build self-efficacy in many tasks, their limitation is their effectiveness which is directly tied to their verisimilitude to reality.

I am not alone in my vision for what can be. Thought leaders and authors including Jane McGonigal who makes the case "Reality is Broken," but offers up ideas which are found in games as possible solutions. McGonigal asks, "What if we started to live our real lives like gamers, lead our real businesses and communities like game designers, and think about solving real-world problems like computer and video game theorists?"

Another great example can be found in physician and leader Dr. James Rosser whose realization that playing video games can improve both the speed and quality of surgeons' performance with certain types of procedures. This realization has opened doors for his further research on the topic, as well as his book *Playin' to Win* which explores the potential of video games to unlock a cultural transformation of "exploration, innovation, and productivity."

These visions are grand in scale and require significant change in how the public views video games and how games are used. I would like to propose allegamy as a generally unexplored opportunity along the way. Allegamy is the low hanging fruit that can enable video games to leverage their inherent strengths as a teaching tool, in a way simple to implement.

I am convinced of the potential for the method of game-based learning when I reflect on the impact both allegory and video games have made on my learning and thought process.

In the pages that follow, I will share with you some of my favorite principles. Ideas which can help you succeed at work and at home, but I will teach these principles through analogy and metaphor contained in a few of my favorite, and I hope your favorite, video games.

Not All Games Are Created Equal

A word of caution: not all video games are created equal. There are games that are poorly designed, poorly programmed, or contain features that harm the overall playability of the game itself. When a game includes flaws of this nature, something interesting tends to happen. Those who play the game begin to complain, using language such as "this game is broken" while highlighting the flaws, or even heavily criticizing the structure and mechanics of the gameplay itself.

It is almost as if there is an instinctive understanding of what makes a game good or bad. One might even call this the underlying principles. Furthermore, I believe it is not necessary to be a long time game player to be able to tell the difference between a great game and a poorly made game. Imagine picking up a video game for the first time. After playing a new game for a few minutes you begin to realize that it is near impossible, or there are elements in the game itself that cause you to lose any hope of succeeding. Very quickly you will realize the game has violated an unspoken principal seated within.

Conversely, if you begin playing a game and there is a sense of hope, or the opportunity to engage in a quick win, you will feel progress or accomplishment from your effort and engagement will increase. Engagement is then maintained by escalating challenges and increasing rewards that scale with your progress within the game.

Balance And Competition

Like many gamers, the player may not even be aware (at least actively) that principles are being adhered to, but if something were to change the structure, or the rules suddenly switched, the impact would be obvious and the backlash immediate. As video games become more dependent on online features and updates to the game can happen through patches live downloads, rebalancing existing games has become more common. This is probably most noticeable in the genre of fighting games, where in competition character balance is important, especially for competition at a high-level.

Beyond fighting games, competitive video game tournaments are part of the rise of "eSports." For example, *Defense of the Ancients* is hosting an annual competitions: the International DotA 2 Championships in Seattle, Washington where the prize pool is almost $11 Million dollars! With over 32 million viewers watching the final 2013 *League of Legends* championship it is no wonder that universities have begun offering scholarships for students who join college video game teams.

With significant money and prestige at stake, it is understandable that players expect, or even demand, a fair and balanced environment. The same holds true for how people feel about their work, or any other environment that they spend a significant amount of time or effort contributing to. The key focus area is to carefully consider: what are the elements that contribute to a good or successful experience within the gaming environment? What are the "must have" success factors and their corresponding principles? Then, how do we help individuals connect the dots between how the behaviors, concepts, and principles that they employed within the video game space, also hold true and have real world application, not just in work, but interactions with other people, in relationships, and even in parenting?

Looking For A Way To Connect The Dots

I find it fascinating that so many values or morals embraced in the classic traditions are equally important to being successful within games. When you look at the morals found within Aesop's fables you can begin to connect the dots and draw the lines back to the video game experience, but a thoughtful approach is required.

Now these principles, ideas, and strategies are only useful if you actually put them to use. If you hold an inventory of the best items in your favorite role-playing game, but you never use them, you might as well not have them at all. If you play a modern fighting game and a powerful super move is saved up, but you never activate it, it does you no good.

Several different methods for using video games to teach have been proposed and researched, but there is much work that remains to truly connect lessons learned in video games with application to success in the professional world. The particular approach I propose is targeted to a specific group of individuals: the game player who is also a professional. With the rich mythology contained in video games, the significant time investment in playing as a down payment, and the positioning as a working adult in their twenties, thirties, or forties, this particular demographic is poised for accelerated growth of the soft skills that are in the greatest demand in our current century.

Music and literature benefit from hundreds of years of refinement, and even the motion picture industry has existed over a century. By comparison, video games are still very much in their infancy, yet their progress in such a short time is impressive, surpassed only by the potential to become an even greater vehicle for human communication and interaction than they are today. I believe the approach of allegamy can further establish video games as a powerful tool that can be used for tremendous growth and development while being enjoyable in a capacity unrivaled by any other format in existence.

True to the philosophy of the approach itself, modern technology is integrated with a classic approach to create Allegamy.

Allegamy

Syllabification: al·le·ga·my

Pronunciation: /ˈalə ˌgāmē /

Definition: The Interpretation of a video game to reveal a hidden meaning, typically a personal development or moral one.

ALLEGAMY IN PRACTICE

"Most people think time is like a river that flows swift and sure in one direction, but I have seen the face of time and can tell you they are wrong. Time is like an ocean in a storm. You may wonder who I am and why I say this. Sit down, and I will tell you a tale like none that you have ever heard."

Prince of Persia: The Sands of Time

I am not so arrogant as to think that I am the first individual to realize the connection of video games and their potential through allegory. There exists many examples of allegamy "in the wild," however, I have not seen an attempt at codifying this technique. I suspect that individuals who have identified the great potential that video games offer for teaching and communicating a message of great value have wrestled with exactly how to leverage allegory and video games together.

The nature of video games is so broad that isolating personal experience, and even degree of engagement, is challenging, but a few successful examples can illustrate the potential.

The following examples are only a sample of the many that could be cited, but represent the range of vehicles that allegamy can leverage to infuse learning, both knowingly and unknowingly. Examples include a parallel understanding of a video game's story elements to an ancient written text, while others look at the use of remixing existing elements of a game to create something new, while yet another example relies heavily on the individual's personal experience in the game to identify with deeply personal application.

A Musical Allegamy

Led by front man Hans van Vliet, 7bit Hero is a bitpop band based out of Brisbane, Australia. The group's music combines chiptune samples, old-school gaming, as well as live instruments to create an experience unlike any other. A novel aspect to their live performances includes an app that attendees download to their mobile devices and interact with games displayed on screens behind the band while they play. The group has released a music video that is part remix, part video game tribute, and part allegamy.

7bit Hero has taken the theme song from the game *Bubble Bobble* and rewritten it into a modern pop masterpiece. Released in the 1980's for both the arcades and home gaming systems, *Bubble Bobble* is a platform orientated action game where one or two players can take control of brothers Bub or Bob who have been transformed into "Bubble

Dragons" by a curse, as they seek to rescue their kidnapped girlfriends from the villainous Super Drunk.

The once annoying and repetitious song heard throughout the entire game has been turned into something that is quite enjoyable and catchy. Hans van Vliet has layered catchy vocals and well-crafted lyrics to elevate this tune into a true work of art. The lyrics themselves are simple enough as they describe what happens in the game. If one was only to listen to the song itself and read the lyrics, it could be easily dismissed as simply paying tribute to the source material of the game.

The deeper message becomes apparent when you watch the video that accompanies the song. The video creates a new context to interpret the lyrics. As the video starts, we see a young boy playing the game *Bubble Bobble* underneath his bed in a dark room.

He seems to be enjoying himself as the lyrics describe the fantasy world he is entering, hidden away from the world in the safety of his room. Throughout the video, we are given alternating glimpses of the real world and the game itself. At one point we see the boy's father outside his room, knocking on the wall with his cane, dislodging a family portrait in the process. The father then enters the kitchen hobbling along with the cane in one hand and a bottle of alcohol in the other.

We watch as the young boy faces off against the boss of the game, curiously named Super Drunk, but as he overcomes his foe, he is faced with a message that he forgot his friend. The game even prompts him, saying "you need a friend," just as the game *Bubble Bobble* does when you complete the game in one player mode. To unlock the true ending of the game you need to invite someone else to play the game along with you. The ending screen reminds us that this is not the true ending.

At this point in the video, the boy gets up from his game and leaves his room, walking out to the kitchen where his father is seen throwing fruit around the kitchen. Suddenly parallels between *Bubble Bobble* and the world in the video become apparent.

On the table outside the boy's room, we see a display set up with a picture of who we can infer from the portrait to be the boy's mother, surrounded by a cross, flowers, and what looks like an urn. The boy then passes his mother's pink necklace laying on the floor, identical to one found in the game, referenced by the lyric of the song "*I just know you left your pink necklace to help me battle through.*"

As the boy turns the corner into the kitchen, he has to walk around fruit thrown by his father, who has emptied the refrigerator to make room for more alcohol. The boy shouts "*cut it out!*" and the father turns around, hanging his head in shame. The dad proclaims "*I miss her,*" tears flowing like a waterfall down both sides of his face, and then the father and son embrace. Red hearts scroll in the background and viewers are left with a message *"You could help your father! He was controlled by someone! Who is he? No one knows of it!"*

An Emotional Journey

Hans van Vliet and 7bit Hero have done a masterful job of taking us on an emotional journey, providing us with an important and inspirational message in the process - it is amazing how a song that is a tribute to a classic video game can also be an emotional experience in storytelling.

The allegamy behind the video is obvious by the time you reach the end of the song. The boy and his father are both coping with the loss of their mother/wife through addiction: the boy with his video games, and the father with alcohol. Items from the real world are found in the game, with the mother's necklace appearing as a symbol of home and encouragement for the boy, and the candy cane acting as a crutch for the father - interesting note: in the game, a candy cane appears after the character has ridden a bubble 20 times, maybe another allegamy for how much the father has been drinking? The genius of the whole parallel, is that all the items exist in the actual *Bubble Bobble* game: the fruit, necklace, cane, even the cross and the urn resemble in game items. Also, the final boss in the original version is named "Super Drunk" and he throws bottles as a weapon.

When asked about the song's inspiration and subject matter, Hans explained how the loss of a friend's mother to cancer, and his own experience of using video games as a coping mechanism were at the heart of the message. He even makes special note of the game asking you about finding a friend as if it was asking you who your support system is.

A Multimedia Storytelling Experience

Bubble Dragon is a masterful use of video game culture, music, video, and storytelling to deliver an important message: we need to look out for others in our lives who may be battling with addictions of any kind, and lovingly help them. This particular use of allegamy resonates with me as a prime example of how creative individuals like Hans van Vliet and projects like 7bit Hero can provide a different picture of how video games and the gaming culture can be used to convey important messages.

Another interesting perspective appears in what might be part coincidence, part intentional story-telling, and part outcome from localization choices.

Chrono Trigger = The Bible?!?

The game in question is *Chrono Trigger*, a classic and well-loved Japanese role playing game that first appeared in the United States on the Super Nintendo Entertainment System in 1995.

This successful game included the talent of the minds behind the *Final Fantasy* and *Dragon Quest* series, and featured artwork from Akira Toriyama, best known for his work as the manga artist for the *Dragon Ball* franchise. Masato Kato was the script writer for the game, and while he has denied allegory outright, many of the in-game elements have an interesting connection to another famous collection of writings: the Bible.

The Chrono Trigger Testament

At one point, there was an entire website called the Chrono Trigger Testament that was dedicated to examining in detail the parallels between the video game *Chrono Trigger* and the Bible. The exhaustive project examined almost every single character and plot contained within the game, cross-referencing to biblical individuals and events recorded in scripture.

Some examples include:

The main character in the game Crono is seen as an allegory for Jesus Christ, a young man who is living with his mother in a normal village but with no mention at all of a father (virgin birth?), which is odd given that many other role playing game of the same time did feature a father, or at least a story explaining his absence.

Once venturing out on his quest, we see Crono grow as a hero, leading a group of followers, and performing "miracles," such as feeding an entire army with a single meal just like Jesus fed over 5000 with five loaves and two fish, or resurrecting a close friend: Robo (Lazarus). The game even includes three wise men who each give Crono a gift, and thanks in part to localization, each of the wise men bears the name of the traditional names given to the three biblical wise men: Balthasar, Gaspar, and Melchior.

If you dig deep enough, and have an open mind, you may even find an instance of Crono walking on the water, delivering an equivalent to the Sermon on the Mount, and some very specific parallels to the end of time in the book of Revelation, all with apparent representation within the game's narrative.

The final events of the game are what most builds the case for the allegamy of *Chrono Trigger*. The events that led up to Jesus' death and Crono's both follow a similar path. Both have a "Last Supper" celebrated before being betrayed by a friend, then are falsely accused by trial, and turned over to be executed. The parallels are all here: the body in charge of the trial are dressed in clothing similar to what the Pharisees wore, and even one specific individual from this group named Pierre who stands up for Crono, who might as well be named "Nicodemus."

Eventually, Crono ends up sacrificing his life to save his friends, dying in a position with his arms outstretched stretched, soon followed by his resurrection. After his resurrection, Crono overcomes the evil Lagos and Queen Zeal before returning to heaven, either by floating away while holding a bunch of balloons, or flying away onboard the flying machine, the Epoch.

The quantity and specificity of these parallels spawned an episode of *Game Theory* that has garnered almost 2 million views, and detailed even further the interesting parallels between the Bible and *Chrono Trigger*, the video game.

Is *Chrono Trigger* an allegamy for the Bible? My guess is, not on purpose.

A Spiritual Journey

Perhaps one of the strongest examples I could cite as an intentional allegamy, is found in the game *Journey*. Originally released exclusively on the Playstation network in 2012 and published by Thatgamecompany, the game *Journey* is yet another masterpiece by Jenova Chen, who is responsible for the games *flOw* and *Flower*. At its core, *Journey* is a playable illustration of Joseph Campbell's *The Hero's Journey,* or *monomyth,* an identified framework that exists across cultures and time periods stretching back to early recorded history up through current narratives like *Star Wars* and *The Matrix.*

Campbell provides a summary definition of the pattern: "A hero ventures forth from the world of common day into a region of supernatural wonder: fabulous forces are then encountered and a decisive victory is won: the hero comes back from this mysterious adventure with the power to bestow boons on his fellow man."

Each segment of the story is further distilled to key milestones that are commonly present, but their absence does not break from the summary above. The stages explicitly experienced in the game *Journey* are as follows:

The Ordinary World

The hero of the game is seen sitting on the edge of a desert, seemingly at home and resting comfortably. It is not clear how they got there, but there is a sense of ease.

The Call to Adventure

A shooting star, or blazing object of some kind flies overhead, landing in a distant area outside of the players view.

Refusal of the Call

The hero stands up, but does not automatically move forward - it is up to the player to now move on ahead or remain where they are.

Meeting with the Mentor

As the hero progresses through the game, they encounter a larger individual, clothed in white robes who allows them to see parts of the upcoming challenges that await the hero.

Crossing the Threshold

The first area of the game concludes with the hero entering a large door that closes behind them. In fact, an in-game trophy that is named "Threshold" is awarded for completing special conditions within one of the early areas in the game.

Tests, Allies, and Enemies

There are puzzles and areas to explore throughout the game, if you are playing online you will most likely meet another player on a journey just like yours, and you will face large stone dragons or guardians starting near the middle of the game.

Approach

The hero and their on line ally prepare for the next leg of the journey by collecting symbols that increase their ability to fly or glide in the game and learn ways of interacting with the environment that will serve them well in the final areas of the journey.

The Ordeal

The greatest fear or challenge is faced in the game around the midpoint, in the underground caves where the hero first meets the guardians/dragons who have come to life, previously only seen as remains or depicted in paintings on the walls.

The Reward

The game does not have one specific item or treasure that is collected, but as the game progresses, the hero has increased their ability to fly or glide, visually represented by the length of their scarf. If the guardian/dragon comes into contact with the hero, this ability is permanently reduced - a heavy and irreversible penalty.

The Road Back

A chase scene happens at the end of the underground area, where several guardians/dragons chase the hero who narrowly escapes into a safe area.

The Resurrection

The hero is tested with more difficult challenges than ever faced: many guardians/dragons, snow conditions that slow the player down, powerful wind that can undo progress the hero has made, and an uphill ascent in the snow that seems to lead to the hero's death. The hero then rises up and is empowered with immense flight abilities in an area that is heaven like and filled with joyful visuals. The hero finally arrives at the top of the mountain - the journey may be complete, but one last part remains.

Return with the Elixir

The hero leaves the mountaintop clothed in their resurrected garb and upgraded scarf, appearing like a shooting star, flying across the landscape of all the areas traveled on the journey, until they fly overhead of another player sitting on the dunes where the hero had begun their own journey.

Making The Journey Your Own

What makes the game *Journey* such a powerful experience is that in the medium of a video game, the player is controlling the pacing of the journey, making the choices that impact the story arc. If the hero wishes to explore the desert and discover the secrets of the game, they can choose to do so. If the player prefers to rush through the areas, driven to accomplish the adventure as fast as possible, this is also within their control. Even the music responds to the player, changing and advancing as the hero progresses.

I find it hard to overemphasize the possibility of personal impact with this particular game. Prior to my "first journey" I would never have fully embraced the idea that a video game can truly be a spiritual experience, but I challenge you not to be moved by playing through the game in one, uninterrupted sitting. In less than two hours, I was able to experience all the elements of Joseph Campbell's identified *Hero's Journey*, culminating in a vicarious death and re-birth more powerful that I have ever experienced while reading a book or watching a movie. Yes, it brought tears to my eyes. Even thinking about it now, I can feel the emotions stirring inside me. This is the power that still remains mostly untapped in the medium of video games. In an interview with the *GamesChurch Podcast*, journalist Patrick Stafford mentioned that *Journey* was the game that most inspired him to reflect on his own faith, labeling the game as perhaps "the most spiritual game in the market."

Unplanned Events on the Journey

While it can be easy to dismiss video games as a source for allegory based on the subjective experience, consider some reflections that I personally made while playing the game.

Who Are You Following?

While in the desert area of *Journey*, I encountered another player. I watched as they ran off, and the speed and intention they used led me to believe that they knew something I did not. I immediately began to follow them. We kept moving across the sand dunes at full pace, over and across ridges, but never encountering anything of interest. This continued for about 10 minutes until we reached an area where the wind blew so hard that we could not advance any further. At this point, the other character sat down and disappeared. After following all this time, trusting them, hoping to discover something useful or important, they simply left. The other player literally disconnected, leaving me alone in the middle of a desert. I had given up my desired path, and now I was so far away from the point where I started that I didn't even know how to start making my way back to where I began.

I have felt the same way in life. Sometimes we chase after other's dreams, or follow in their footsteps, thinking that somehow we will be better off for it. We assume this so-called "expert" has knowledge that we do not possess. Then when we think the answer we have been looking for is about to arrive, we find out that we are alone.

Worse yet we are so far from the place in life where we wanted to be, and now the reason for being here is gone too. I've seen this happen with friends, co-workers, and I have even felt it myself. The sense of being abandoned, forgotten, or left by our self, is really a heavy burden. We can take this allegamical lesson as a reminder to be cautious the next time we are tempted to follow the crowd, or even another individual. We must remember that we are on a journey of our own. If we spend our lives following, we end up in places we do not know, do not want to be, and do not know how to leave.

And when we do leave, we experience the pain and frustration of lost time, effort, energy, and even a little (or big) piece of who we are. Sure it can be lonely to go out on our own, but we cannot let loneliness be the reason for diverting our life's journey. If you are not actively pursuing your own path, then you are spending your life helping others chase their dreams. Don't get me wrong, I am not saying to turn your back on everyone else. There is something fulfilling about helping others be successful - I am all for that. However, this cannot be at the expense of your own calling and purpose.

Now the positive side of this exists as well. There were many times that another player was able to show me a location I did not know about. In the game *Journey*, players who are on a second, third, or fourth play through have different symbols on their cloak. Finding an individual with these symbols, or one who has a long scarf showing that they have picked up numerous power ups along the way, would be a hint that this individual might be able to help you in your own journey.

However, capacity or knowledge does not equal willingness to assist. If a person is unwilling to act as a mentor, you can still observe what they do. By observing their behaviors and actions we can follow in their footsteps and learn along the way.

This is another profound example of actions speaking louder than words.

Journeys May Align But Only For A Season

Along the same lines, other people come and go throughout our lives, with research demonstrating that we may lose up to half of our current friends every seven years. There are many reasons for this, but if you look at the friends you spend time with today, chances are there are many different people in your circle than were there 7 years ago. I think about my own journey and consider how milestones have changed the members of my "inner circle."

When we are young, we are close to our neighbors and classmates in school. Once we enter the workforce, a change begins as we meet a new circle where we spend a large portion of our time. We are now spending more time with people who share a different interest, usually some commonality in the industry we are employed in.

I noticed the next big change when my wife and I were married. We spend much more time with other married couples, and the time spent with friends who were single dramatically decreased. After 8 years of marriage, my wife and I had a baby. Having a baby changes so much, as any parents out there can attest to. With the addition to our family, we have been introduced to an entirely new set of friends and we find ourselves spending a lot of time with people that we did not even know just a few years ago.

When we are younger, we tend to worry about what our peers will think about us, only to realize a few years later, the people we were so concerned about impressing are no longer in our lives. I understand that Facebook and other social media platforms have reshaped this concept a bit, as I have been able to get back in touch with people I knew from my childhood, but by in large, I am not spending my time with them as much as simply reconnecting.

This concept is mirrored in the game of *Journey*. While the experience is multiplayer in nature, there is no set arrangement that keeps the players together. When one player takes a different direction, press ahead, or stay behind and explore, the other player can remain by their side or move on with their own journey. Each time a player passes through the door at the end of the each area in the game, the opportunity to connect with a new player happens.

In *Journey*, you can encounter a half dozen other players in the course of your own journey, and it is not until the very end that you have a chance to know anything about them. Once you complete the game, a single screen displays the user names of the individuals you have shared the experience with. It is almost like sitting down at the end of your life and flipping through a photo album or school year book to remember the individuals who have touched your life. This somber reminder happens after the part of the game that had the most meaningful impact on me.

The End of a Journey

Orson Wells said: "We're born alone, we live alone, we die alone. Only through our love and friendship can we create the illusion for the moment that we're not alone."

This holds true both in life and in the game of *Journey*. As the player reaches the end of the game on their final approach to the snowy summit, everything begins to slow down. Staying close to the other player becomes almost impossible. Eventually each of you end up on your own and collapse in the snow as the screen fades out to white.

And then silence. When your eyes refocus you are surrounded by light and encircled by white robed ancestors present to welcome you into the next life.

My best interpretation of this moment is an arrival into heaven, where you are surrounded by light and clear blue skies. In the *Journey* commentary, founder of Thatgamecompany, Jenova Chen pointed out that the bright blue skies were reserved specifically for this portion of the game to further magnify the emotion of the moment. Everything that was interesting and fun is re-created in a new environment where you can move without limits, flying around unrestricted amongst the beauty that is the afterlife of *Journey*. The remarkable soundtrack composed by Austin Wintory continues to respond to the player in a dynamic fashion, reaching a crescendo just before landing atop the final summit, symbolizing the end of the journey.

It is hard to do justice to or overstate the impact this game and moment had on me. This moment was one of spiritual transcendence, much like the essence of what author C.S. Lewis describes as "Joy" - a taste or touch of the greatness that is Heaven only enough to inspire or move us and give us the hope for the joy what could one day be. He best describes this idea in *Surprised By Joy*, saying: "All Joy reminds. It is never a possession, always a desire for something longer ago or further away or still 'about to be'." The moment also puts to rest the debate as to whether or not video games can be considered art.

Before her involvement with the creation of *Journey*, co-founder of Thatgamecompany, Kellee Santiago responded to film critic Roger Ebert's opinion that video games could not be considered art, making a well thought out case publically. As is often the case with persuasive arguments, Kellee's most irrefutable point was made through actions, not just words. Simply playing the game *Journey* is enough to squelch opposition to the notion that games can truly be art.

Now of course, it is unrealistic to expect that every individual playing this game could have an experience on the same level or be touched in the same exact way. Personal experience, personality, belief systems, and world view all intersect and interact with experiential video game play.   This facet is both the immense strength and possible weakness found within the media of video games.

The Strength And Weakness Of Interactivity

Allegory within movies and books is a fixed experience when compared to a video game tale. Books and movies can direct the attention of the individual, forcing them to notice specific details, plot points, and take them down a specific path. Excellent video games thrive on player participation, decision making, and self-direction. Writer, game designer, and video game industry executive

Jeff Tidball points out that,"The nature of games—that their storylines are flexible—is at odds with allegory."

I agree that this feature is a challenge, but it is also the greatest area for opportunity and strength in crafting a purposeful allegory/video game. We have just examined the features of the Campbell's The Hero's Journey that appear in Thatgamecompany's *Journey*, but the individual experience also allows for additional experiences that can be self-interpreted.

The sticking point of self-interpretation, is that it is too personal to create a reliable outcome. The careful balance for a video game maker is creating both a personal and self-directed experience, while still drawing attention to the important elements of the game. Readers or movie watchers can always skip ahead a chapter or fast forward through a segment of a book or movie, but as long as you follow along the established path, you will encounter the required plot elements.

Video games are often designed to make it required for the player to do certain things, but many times there are ways around this, intentionally or unintentionally. Imagine watching a movie, only to have it freeze in the final 15 minutes because you missed something in the first half of the movie, and the only way to watch it through to the end would be to restart the entire DVD. Many gamers have experienced this type of discouragement due to poor game design or even a flaw or bug that is exploited.

Thankfully, this is not a problem in most games.

NOT QUITE GAMIFICATION

"In every job that must be done, there is an element of fun. You find the fun, and - SNAP - the job's a game!"

Mary Poppins

"We can do it, just keep your eyes upon the prize."

Parappa, Parappa the Rapper

Gamification is a concept that still has great untapped potential and is a very real part of the workforce and consumer experience today. It is also frequently misunderstood. I am not a gamification expert, but I know the buzz-word laden and gimmick riddled misunderstanding of the concept is rather common in the Human Resources and business side of many organizations. A simplified misunderstanding of gamification typically includes collection of "badges" or a "points" system. While these elements are two commonly used components of gamification, they are often misused and result in poor or limited outcomes when not included as part of a larger system.

Gamification expert, Gabe Zichermann provides a meaningful working definition: "Gamification is the process of using Game Thinking and Game Dynamics to Engage Audiences and Solve Problems." The key here is on solving problems and engaging the audience. In the proper context, badges and points make sense, and do indeed drive engagement. However, placing arbitrary points in the incorrect context will only create confusion at best, and cynicism or disengagement at worst.

Dan Pink, author of *Drive: The Surprising Truth About What Motivates Us* points out the additional danger that lies in using concepts like gamification as an extrinsic motivator: "The problem with making an extrinsic reward the only destination that matters is that some people will choose the quickest route there, even if it means taking the low road." This type of behavior has been implicit in many modern business scandals.

The key to gamification is natural fit. As with any intervention, one must be responsible and ask important questions, such as "does this encourage the behaviors we want to see?" The original sources for the inspiration behind gamification techniques work well because they were an integral part of the game itself, not a shoehorned feature or game play mechanic. Many times, less is more.

Consider that not every video game has a point system, character levels, or unlockable equipment. For the game mechanic to be successful, it has to be appropriate. Otherwise, it is just a distraction.

Modern games have implemented a universal system for in game trophies or achievements, and in some cases it is very apparent that achievements only exist out of necessity. There have been many games where I receive a notification that I have been awarded an achievement simply for completing a level, starting a game, or just playing a game for a second time. These are not meaningful and are typically met with disinterest, apathy, or sarcastic humor. Proof that even gamification of games does not work when the goal does not align with the desired outcomes.

The Holy Grail Of Gamification

Do you know that feeling you get when you are totally absorbed in an activity you love—even to the point of completely losing track of the time? That sense is amazing, but often hard to replicate.

Mihaly Csikszentmihalyi, a psychologist and professor of psychology at Claremont Graduate University in Claremont, California, describes this condition as "flow" in his book *Flow: The Psychology of Optimal Experience.*

"The state in which people are so involved in an activity that nothing else seems to matter; the experience itself is so enjoyable that people will do it even at great cost, for the sheer sake of doing it," he writes.

Video games are often cited as one of the most quickly accessed sources of flow. There's even a game called *flOw* that pays homage to Csikszentmihalyi. Achieving a state of flow is part of what makes playing video games so enjoyable. This is also one of the most desired byproducts of successful gamification.

The following is an example of how gamification and game mechanics can be applied to inspire flow in a typical office or desk based profession.

Engaging Flow In The Workplace

Minimize Visual Distractions

One contributing factor to flow is the singularity of focus—you can achieve this by shutting out interruptions. The type of work you do may have some built-in limitations, but choose instead to focus on the areas you can control. Many video games have very elegant information displays that typically do a great job of helping you focus only on the numbers that matter. Some ways you can implement this feature in the workspace might include:

- Limit multitasking by shutting down every application you do not need

- Turn off any notifications that are not essential

- Put your cell phone out of sight

- Clear off your desk space

- De-clutter everything within your field of vision

The goal here is if you can see it, it should relate directly to what you are doing. While a clean workspace is not exclusive video games, the best games are purpose driven and intentional in this regard, so this principle is ideal to implement in any workplace or profession.

Select The Soundtrack

One of my favorite sources of video game nostalgia is the audio that accompanies many top games. The quality of video game music has advanced dramatically since the original bleeps and bloops of arcade games like *Donkey Kong* and *Space Invaders*.

Many video game soundtracks are stand-alone works of art in their own right, but I especially recommend soundtracks from role-playing games like the *Final Fantasy* game series. The ideal works are sweeping orchestral pieces that fit the bill for being both pleasing to listen to and are noninvasive. This is the perfect combination for productivity-inducing background music.

Christofer Karltorp, CEO of Zerply, has been successfully using the soundtracks to video games to boost focus and productivity during work time, refining his approach to the point of using more ambient pieces for certain types of project work, or employing high energy songs like the music of *Street Fighter* to tear through emails quickly. In an article from *FastCompany*, he makes a comment key to the music's strength "It is there in the background. It doesn't get too intrusive, it keeps you going, and usually stays on a positive tone, too, which I found is important."

Headsets are a good idea for listening where permitted, but given the quality and general appeal of many RPG soundtracks, a well-selected play list may even win over the entire office for public listening.

Enforce Time Limits

A timer counting down creates a sense of urgency. Many video games have built-in time limits that specific tasks must be completed within. The presence of a time-tracking system also allows for better management of time resources, and can help keep a project on track. The motivation produced is as important as the evasion of procrastination. A study conducted by social network company Draugiem Group determined the ideal time for productivity is 52 minutes of focused intensity, followed by 17 minutes of break time. This cycle allows for focused and purposeful activity with an anticipated break at the end.

If you—or your boss—are concerned about frequent 17-minute breaks throughout the day, consider the time normally spent on non-work activities like restroom breaks, meals, making coffee, and commuting from meetings. Build those activities into non-work intervals and then reduce the break down to 10 minutes if time is still an issue.

Tracking the time should be simple. Apps or programs like Marinara Timer will allow you to set a timer for a specific period of your choosing. So, you can take the guesswork out of when to set your next alarm, and provide a visual reminder of the countdown.

Create Multiple Stages

Take the concept of breaking work into segments to the next level. Video games like the classic *Super Mario World* offer players an experience that almost reaches 100 stages. What makes this manageable is the experience is broken up into 96 parts spread across nine worlds— inclusive of bonus worlds—each with their own checkpoints. Applying the tactics discussed in the timer suggestion, milestones can be given their own time limits which will create an opportunity to experience the joys of a win for each step in the process.

The key here is to carefully plan out your steps:

- Identify your goal

- Create a list of key milestones

- Put them into a calendar

- Get started

Reward Yourself For Success

Another important key to productivity is recognition. Video games are especially good at rewarding and recognizing positive behaviors and results. Part of this lies in the programming. Many modern games allow for in-game trophies or achievements for completing certain tasks, usually giving specific details how to accomplish the feat. Unlike the typical workplace when the conditions are met, the award is immediately received every time.

Consistency is much easier in a virtual world, where rewards and achievements can be doled out through an automated process, since this minimizes the likelihood good behavior will fail to be recognized, or poor performance will go unnoticed. This is part of the challenge managers face when overseeing groups in the workplace.

For personal productivity, establish a set of prizes you will award yourself with upon completion of a task or milestone. The best part about managing yourself this way is you know what matters most. I know I will not reward myself with watching a reality TV show because that holds no motivation for me to strive toward. However, a cup of coffee, a sushi dinner, or even a few laughs via YouTube will give me something to look forward to.

These are just five examples of simple techniques that can be used in almost any workplace to boost engagement, productivity and flow. I am not an expert on gamification, but I am hopeful for the potential of the approach.

With some of the keys of gamification detailed, the next approach that holds significant potential for learning and application derived from video games involves "connecting the dots." What will work in video games and what can also work in the real world is not always obvious. If approached with an open mind, the applications are near endless to the discriminating individual as we examine how successful behaviors in one realm can also lead to success in another. At the core of this idea are underlying principles. Understanding these principles are the key to unlocking the immense possibilities that video games have for teaching, developing, and applying transferable skills.

PART II: TRANSFERRABLE SKILLS

CONNECTING THE DOTS

"Knowing it in your head doesn't mean much if you don't act on it."

Sanae Hanekoma, The World Ends With You

When I asked best-selling author Simon Sinek what he had learned from video games, he offered an interesting reply: "It's difficult to know where our lessons come from." Part of what I believe makes understanding where learning comes from it so difficult is that it is often a combination of various sources that refine our understanding over time. We observe, make presumptions, and look for additional information to confirm or deny our hypothesis.

Our understanding of the world around us is made easier, if not simpler, through principles. Along these lines, I wish to propose a case that principles can be taught or reinforced in video games, and then can instruct and teach real life success. An idea I have seen hinted at, but not yet fully realized is the potential for transferrable skills, specifically skills video games develop, that can be applied to work, school, or everyday situations. Let us consider for a moment a few core concepts.

Concept One: Principles Transcend The Media In Which They Appear

One definition of principle given by Merriam-Webster is interesting in setting the stage for the point I wish to make: "the laws or facts of nature underlying the working of an artificial device." In this definition, the fact that a device is artificial does not exempt it from being subject to the laws or facts of nature. In the same way, many video games reflect underlying principles of reality. If the game follows these principles, and the game player can succeed in the video game subject to these principles, might it not be possible that these same actions or activities can lead to success in the workplace, school, or life itself?

What if success in one realm could serve as a pattern for success in another?

Concept Two: At The Heart Of Every Game Is A Problem-Solving Simulator

Video games are full of problems. The world needs saving. The villain needs to be stopped. This item must be collected, or that task must be completed. A neighbor in the village needs you to take the empty bottle to the farmer to fill it full of milk, who then asks you to milk the cow yourself. Sounds like work. Did I mention that evil orcs are trying to kill you while you are milking the cow? Problem solving at its finest. The time most players of *The Legend of Zelda* series have spent either cutting down grass or fishing is down right mind numbing.

Ironically, many who enjoy video games will spend the day at work or school, challenged by problem solving scenarios, difficult choices, or mindless and repetitive tasks, only to come home looking forward to… solving problems, making difficult choices, and completing repetitious tasks in a video game.

Why? Because it is fun to win and be successful, and many video games make this much easier than most places of work. Games have the advantages of being designed to keep the player engaged. Can you imagine your boss or employer approaching you with a job description designed to keep you engaged, excited, and challenged at work? Any organization that could do this successfully would have to force their employees to go home every day and mandate they take the weekends off.

The obvious difference here is that job roles are designed with a different purpose. Jobs exist to solve a bigger problem for the employer and the business, not primarily to benefit the employee. In fact, "that's why you get paid" might be the retort of the calloused, traditional business owner. This concept reveals the interesting tension between the "entitlement" that many Millennials display in the workforce and the actual expectations of the job.

Concept Three: You Can Learn Without Knowing It

What excites me about the potential for learning principles from video games, is the possibility it can be done without the learner even being actively aware that they are learning. In a later section, we will take a look at a problem solving approach that discovers how many difficult problems may already be resolved by individuals who are completely unaware they are doing anything different from everyone else. This approach, called Positive Deviance, depends on the problem solver often being ignorant of their own solution, but simply doing things differently because "that's just the way I do it."

Leveling Up Development

Another important component to knowledge is developmental levels. Ken Blanchard's Situational Leadership model includes a specific framework that also addresses individual development. This approach identifies two determinants of both learning and performance: Competence and Commitment.

Competence comprises knowing what to do and how to do it. When playing a video game, the player spends a significant amount of time learning the game. The time spent varies game to game, but each new game brings with it a control scheme, game mechanics, and specific goal within the game. A new player must invest time and work at understanding the "what" and the "how" of the video game to enjoy it. Just because I am highly competitive in *Rival Schools* does not mean I am automatically good at *Power Stone* or *The Last Blade*.

Confidence is developed as belief in one's ability to perform a task or achieve the desired outcome in a successful fashion. I can have confidence that I can successfully complete the first stage in *Battletoads* but lack confidence that I can ever finish the speeder bike stage in the same game. In this way, confidence is specific to a particular task or goal.

What about the skills or abilities that can be learned in one context and applied to another? I have been playing video games for over 30 years, and I would say I have an advantage in learning a video game's play mechanics over someone who is less familiar with video games. This begs the question: do some of the skills or knowledge acquired while playing previous video games aid me in quickly understanding newer games I have yet to experience? If that is true, then what might be the possibility that skills learned in video games can be gained and transferred to life in the same way?

Were this the case (and I believe it is) then these skills would qualify as "transferable skills." Consider that often, transferable skills include the capacity to analyze, store and retrieve information, as well as using past information in new contexts. This is why fans of one genre of video game can often pick up a new game in the same genre with a minimal learning curve.

4 Stages of Mastery

When approaching the subject of mastery, there are four distinct levels to consider (in order): Unconscious Incompetence, Conscious Incompetence, Conscious Competence, and Unconscious Competence.

Unconscious Incompetence

This is the individual who picks up a new video game unlike anything they have ever played. At first they expect to be good at it, only to find that their skills are lacking. They are terrible, the truth be told, but they don't know it yet – hence, the unconscious part of their incompetence.

Conscious Incompetence

This individual openly admits that they do not understand what they are doing, but they are willing to learn. This is a fine place for any beginner to be since there exists an openness to learning and a humility that allows for quicker growth. In this stage we begin to learn how little we know about a subject, or in this case, a game.

Conscious Competence

Next is the individual who is learning and acquiring a good skill set. The rules of the game have set in, but effort is still required to remember button pressing combinations or which spell to use against which enemy. Slowly getting better, and almost there.

Unconscious Competence

The final stage is reserved for the individual who no longer has to think about which button to press or which weapon to select, but can handle quick and complicated responses without even needing to think about it. This is a high degree of mastery.

Transferable Competence

What if we applied the concepts of competence and consciousness to transferable skills? I submit for consideration the individual who has achieved a high level of competence in a transferable skill, but they are unaware that this skill can serve them in a completely different context. This Unconscious Transferable Competence could be the key to unlocking the significant potential of video games to set individuals up for success in reality. Can success in one environment lead to success in another? If principles and transferable skills align, there is a very strong possibility.

10,000 Hours of Gameplay

A key element of being an Unconscious Transferable Competent is a high degree of practice of the skill in question. In Malcolm Gladwell's frequently quoted work *Outliers,* he references the 10,000 hour rule which represents the quantity of time that must be spent studying a subject to be considered an expert. Is it within the realm of possibility that many gamers spend 10,000 hours or more playing video games? Jane McGonigal makes the case that the average young person accomplishes this feat before reaching their 21st birthday.

What exactly are the Unconscious Transferable Competencies that are being developed during these 10,000 hours? A list of skills that resembles the needed skills lacking in leadership to achieve a more dynamic workplace: Strategic Planning, Change Management, Knowledge Sharing, Listening, Innovation, Adaptability, Teamwork, Learning, and Collaboration. If the needed skills are being learned, the million dollar question is why are they not showing up in the workplace?

Concept Four: What You Can Do Only Matters If You Know When To Do It

Once competencies have been built the next step would require an effort of connecting the dots to move from self-efficacy in one realm to self-efficacy in another. To gain and sustain performance, an individual needs to know "what" and "how" (competence), as well as have a belief in his or her abilities (confidence) and a desire to achieve an outcome (motivation). If I am unaware that I am doing something a certain way, then how can I improve my performance?

An example of a skill inherent to video games, but benefits the player through illumination is problem solving and the scientific method.

Successful Problem Solving

Considering that video games are problem solving simulators, what are elements of the required problem solving skills found in video games that can be transferred to real life situations? Could it be possible that Massive Multiplayer Online games (MMOs) like *World of Warcraft* can teach and build efficacy with the scientific method, for example?

One possible starting point for realizing what type of transferable skills exist within games is self-awareness. As we become self-aware of the behaviors that have potential for transferability, the likelihood of noticing more skills that meet this criteria will increase. A good universal set of skills that games teach is discussed at length in *Everything Bad is Good For You* by Steven Johnson where decision-making is observed within video games. How a player seeks, interacts, and decides within the video game can be split into two distinct techniques: probing, and telescoping.

Johnson describes probing as engaging with the environment and actively learning the consequences that specific behaviors create. Essentially this is a real-time interaction within the system, much like trial and error. This is the scientific method that James Paul Gee describes: Probe, Hypothesize, Re-Probe, and rethink approach.

Probing seeks to find the edge or outer limits or boundaries of what the game can do. It is only when you understand the size and shape of the box that you can either think outside the box or learn to be successful within it. The scientific method and its application throughout the video game world can be seen in research by Steinkuehler and Duncan.

In *Scientific Habits of Mind in Virtual Worlds,* Constance Steinkuehler and Sean Duncan discover several remarkable findings among avid fans of Massive Multiplayer Online games.

The research examined the nature of conversations taking place on the official *World of Warcraft* forums. Understanding and application of the scientific method, evaluative thinking, social knowledge construction, systems based reasoning, and model based approaches were identified in this study. Rather intense subjects for what many have dismissed as "just a game."

This in itself is an amazing tool for teaching and understanding a highly transferable skill, yet there remains another skill that is potentially more helpful at the leadership level within organizations and groups - this skill is referred to as Telescoping. Telescoping is when the game player can engage in the ability to track many different tasks and goals that range from immediate and short-term all the way through long-term and global/enterprise level goals. This is not multitasking, but rather project management in a dynamic environment. This skill is key to being successful as a manager, supervisor, or director within an organization, and vital to top executives.

Similar to the example of gamification in the previous chapter, below is an example of how these principles found in video games can be connected to business, professional, and entrepreneurial environments with great success. Take special note how this particular approach varies from gamification.

Three Principles from Video Games For Professionals, Small Businesses and Entrepreneurs

Small businesses and entrepreneurs face many challenges, so why not look for answers from an industry that is designed around overcoming difficulty and a product that has consumers lining up for the latest opportunity to invest time and money for the privilege of solving problems?

Essentially, video games are problem solving simulators that rely on hard work and persistence. Just beneath their digital surface lie countless lessons and success principles that are often overlooked as critics dismiss video games on the account of the notion that games are a waste of time, childish, and source of excessive violence.

How can entrepreneurs and small business owners apply principles from video games to gain an unfair advantage over their competition? Here are three powerful ways that business owners can take their game to the next level.

Set Clear Goals and Establish Quick Wins

To achieve efficiently and effectively, a clear goal is essential. Video games use maps, visual and auditory prompts, and purposeful design to communicate to the player the desired outcome.

A way that video games can help with change efforts is the concept of generating short-term wins. Video game players have all experienced short-term wins. Most good games have them, either explicitly or implicitly, and place them strategically – in particular, at the beginning of the game. Completing the first stage of a game is usually much easier than later stages. This is no accident.

Leaders can harness the power of short-term wins to help make the desired change in their company by considering the following components of an effective short-term win.

· **Short-term wins need to be visible**, verifiable and not just a rumor or hype.

· **Short-term wins need to be unambiguous,** so that stakeholders will all come to the same conclusion. This also helps with how the short-term win can be accomplished, because when there's clarity around what we are doing, how we get there is less important than why we are doing it in the first place.

· **Short-term wins must be linked to the larger change effort.** If the win is completely unrelated to a larger goal or objective, then it doesn't do much good – it is just a distraction.

There are many factors that contribute to the success of short-term wins. They provide a great source of feedback in terms of progress. Think about all the video games that break the experience up into stages, checkpoints, levels and worlds. If we didn't have a way to measure progress in video games, gaming could become tedious, exhausting, or cause us to lose interest. Change expert John Kotter sums up this responsibility in Leading Change, "The job of management is to win in the short term while making sure you're in an even stronger position to win in the future."

Success is Iterative

The video game industry has become quite effective at the concept of iteration, even to a flaw. The title of a recent entry in a popular role playing game series says it all: *Final Fantasy XIII-2*. Thought leader Simon Sinek commented on iteration in the gaming industry when asked about a recent visit to the American Headquarters of video game titan Nintendo. "We think innovation is when we invent great products, and what we forget is that the best ones are always iterative," he says.

He went on to describe that outside the Nintendo cafeteria, games throughout the company's history are on display. Visitors can observe the various iterations of gaming systems and gain a clear understanding of progress. Sinek clarifies: "In other words, they didn't start by imagining the Game Boy, they started with a huge thing and thought 'how can we improve upon this?' And so this is really what innovation is, it is about how to take something that you have and make a continuous system of improvement."

Remember To Save

Saving progress in a video game has become essential, especially as the length and complexity of video games have increased. Saving your game is all about picking up where you left off. We spend hours working, collecting, progressing, and advancing, so naturally, we don't want to start over from the very beginning.

The idea here is to create backups for your most important assets, but there is also a more personal takeaway. Have you ever made the same mistake over and over again, perhaps even telling yourself "I've learned my lesson this time," only to find yourself falling into the same situation again? Consider how to capture the lessons learned and ideas, with the most simple of tools being a written journal. Successful world leaders, executives, and professionals from all industries can see significant benefits from keeping a work journal.

Video games provide a dynamic source for learning principles that can be applied in a wide range of situations. Video games provide an excellent environment for experimentation with low risk, and the savvy business owner will see the potential of putting these lessons into play.

Moving From General To Specific

General knowledge is useful, but to see significant benefits, knowledge should become personal and specific. The rest of this book is structured to provide targeted examples of how personal development, business knowledge, and leadership skills can be learned through allegamy, connecting the dots, and Unconscious Transferable Competence.

Specifically, I will address the top identified skills that are highest in demand yet lacking in leadership within organizations: Strategic Planning, Adaptability, Change Management, Personal Accountability, Innovation, Strengths based development, Learning, Communication, Listening, Team building, Collaboration, Knowledge Sharing, Persistence and Grit.

STRATEGIC PLANNING

"We come into this world with our eyes closed. And most of us choose to live our whole lives that way."

Call of Duty: Advanced Warfare

It was a terrible feeling, I literally froze.

My palms were sweating, my heart was beating fast, and my mouth went dry. I could barely speak.

The moderator repeated the question: "Which team do you choose?"

I just couldn't seem to think clearly. I missed the chance to select my first choice of teams. I didn't know what to do. I hadn't thought this far ahead. I never stopped to ask myself "what if I don't have the chance to choose the Chicago Bulls?"

"Charlotte," I mumbled, coming up with the best answer I could in the moment.

81

The truth is it didn't matter what team I selected. I had already lost.

****

1994 was a great year for me. It meant the opportunity to participate in the Blockbuster Video World Game Championships.   For those who are not familiar, starting in 1994 and repeating the following year, Blockbuster Video hosted a video game competition across the USA. Some of you might also remember a movie named The Wizard. While essentially a 90 minute long commercial for Nintendo games and products, Fred Savage plays the lead in the story about a video game competition that also included the North American unveiling of *Super Mario Brothers 3*.

And it featured the Powerglove. *It is so Bad.*

The Blockbuster Video World Game Championship was a lot like that movie, only minus the Powerglove (which really was bad, and not in the 1980s/Michael Jackson way). The tournament was categorized by the two competing consoles of the time: Sega Genesis or Super Nintendo. Each of the competitors in the championship were given a certain amount of time to achieve the highest score possible across three games.

On the Super Nintendo system the games were in *NBA Jam, Teenage Mutant Ninja Turtles: Tournament Fighters*, and *Clay Fighter*. The individual who achieved the highest score from each store for their console of choice advanced to the finals held in Fort Lauderdale, Florida. I won the Super Nintendo division from my local store in Royal Palm Beach, and I even had my picture displayed in the local newspaper. You can only imagine how thrilled I was to have my picture in the local paper for winning at video games. Blockbuster Video sweetened the deal by providing winners a handful of various giveaways: cool little prizes including a metal pin, t-shirt and a hat with the Blockbuster World Game Championship logo printed on them.

This experience was incredible, and I had the great fortune to make friends with the winner of the Super Nintendo category for another local store in Wellington, Florida. We both traveled down to the tournament in Fort Lauderdale, Florida in my parent's minivan, not knowing what expect.

When we arrived, we discovered that all competitors would play on the large stage at the front of the room, in a head-to-head game of NBA Jam. My friend and I wished each other luck and parted ways. When I took the stage, I was seated next to my competitor in front of a large TV. I am pretty sure he was a year or two younger than me and obviously wasn't that cool since he wore his Blockbuster hat to the Blockbuster tournament. Kids.

The Blockbuster moderator approached both of us and asked my competitor which team he would prefer to use. He answered "the Chicago Bulls," and the moderator locked in his selection. The moderator then asked me which team I wanted. I didn't know what to say.

Wait. Hold on, that was my team, I thought.

You see, I was convinced that the Chicago Bulls had the advantage over every other team. I had only played matches against the computer up to this point, so I naturally assumed that I would be playing as Chicago. I was unprepared for this situation, and it did not occur to me that I could contest his choice. My lack of a "plan B" threw off my game so much I didn't even know who to select as my next choice for a team. I impulsively choose Charlotte as my selection, and the game began.

Throughout the whole game I found myself distracted by the question "what would've happened if I had *my* team?" Every shot I missed, I caught myself thinking, "If I had Chicago, I would've made that shot." Every pass that was intercepted, I told myself "He only got that ball because he's playing as the Bulls." I came up with one excuse after another, blaming everything that went wrong on team selection. The final buzzer of the game sounded. It was over.

I ended up losing by four points.

I was so disappointed. As I looked back at everything that happened I noticed something interesting. The team selection meant little in the end. There was a bigger issue involved in my loss that day. If I had prepared better and asked myself the question "What is my plan B? What will I do if the other guy selects Chicago?" the outcome may have been very different.

I would have been better equipped to make a good choice, and more importantly I would not have been so emotionally shaken up when I did not have things go "my way." This was a high pressure situation where competitors were on a stage in front of a large audience, something I wasn't used to at the age of 14. It was far more pressure than I felt sitting in my living room playing video games with friends. It was even more pressure than I felt inside my local Blockbuster store while qualifying for the finals.

A Matter Of Tactics

It was not until many years later that I found myself enjoying a game that could have better prepared me with the strategies I needed to be successful. The genre of Turn-Based Strategy games (and its cousin, Real Time Strategy games) have been around for quite a while, but it was not until I played *Final Fantasy Tactics* that I learned to appreciate this class of video game. I had played chess and other strategy based board games before, but nothing of equal complexity. Chess has only 6 different types of pieces. *Final Fantasy Tactics* has 20 basic jobs (classes) with the total count of playable/non-playable classes totaling 56. Each job can also obtain and equip unique skills and equipment, further multiplying the complexity of any given match. Besides the various classes, each member of your team gains experience and grows in their abilities as you use them to play matches.

I have spent countless hours developing and growing different members of my team, only to lose one permanently from the game through poor choices or timing. The game uses an isometric (3/4th overhead) view with a grid laid overtop the field. Like a game of chess, players take turns moving their pieces around the board, positioning for an advantage, in an effort to defeat the opposing player. Beyond the compelling game play and sophisticated mechanics, the game is story driven with a medieval/fantasy backdrop filled with political and social duress.

Eventually I enjoyed other strategy games like *Command and Conquer* and *Starcraft*. This style of gaming is demanding that the players think at a very high strategic level while making split second decisions that can impact their entire match.

Thinking Ahead In Life

In work, school, or just going about your day, you may have a plan A or a preferred choice, but what if things don't go the way you want them to go? How many other people want that close parking space at the store? And every time you enter a contest – how many others think they should win, too?

More importantly, how will you handle the situation when you do not get your first choice? I have seen many people handle situations very poorly when they don't get their way. Think about the last time you were in a store or some other public place, and a small child was throwing a temper tantrum. Embarrassing, right? As uncomfortable as it is to watch a child have a small meltdown, it is even more problematic for an adult. Sure, there are less tears, screaming, and flailing of limbs – but not always.

In the unfortunate case of the adult temper tantrum, the source of the problem is the same as in the toddler: poor thinking. This idea that exists in the mind that "I will always get my way" is the source of so much frustration and bad behavior. While I am not completely sure of where this way of thinking comes from, I can tell you I suffer from it, just like many others you know, perhaps even yourself. This very rigid way of thinking is unhelpful for many reasons, not the least of which is the triggering of our fight or flight mechanism.

87

One way to set ourselves up for success, is to create better balance. Work/life balance is a term that is kicked around in organizations looking to improve their employee experience, but it is ultimately up to each of us to balance our own schedule.

Resource Management Of Time

We all wear many hats, I know I have a few myself: Husband, Father, Brother, Son, Friend, Manager, Employee, Entrepreneur, Blogger, Gamer -just to name a few. I am sure you have a few responsibilities of your own. Everyone seems to struggle to find work/life balance. And as far as I know, there is no Game Genie for achieving work life balance to give you infinite time and resources.

So how do I keep it all balanced?

The truth is, sometimes I don't. But here is a strategy and a tool that can change your life and give you a peace of mind more successfully than anything else that I have tried. First, we need to change how we look at time.

It is often said that, "time is money."

This principle holds true, when we are talking about time or money: a budget will tell your money where to go, a schedule will tell your time where you want it to go. Imagine a business that does not budget its expenses. It is not open any longer. No matter how much money you have, you need a budget. And you should approach time the same way.

The problem is, that we don't budget time properly. We overlook things we cannot control, and then we forget to make time for the things that are most important to us. There never is enough time to do it all, but you can spend your time on the things that matter most to you.

Work Life Balance Is Like Inventory Management While Surrounded by Zombies

I recommend creating an "ideal week" calendar. This will not be perfect, and you will probably never have a week like this, but the value is to think about what is most important, and then assigning time for those activities. My approach is based on a framework provided by President and CEO of Intentional Leadership, Michael Hyatt.

Completing this exercise is more difficult than a game of *Dark Souls*. It actually feels like managing your inventory in *Resident Evil 4*. The Resident Evil series always included item scarcity and inventory limits in the games as additional challenges (in case the zombies were not enough). In *RE4*, you guide Leon S. Kennedy in a more action oriented take on the survival horror franchise. Leon's inventory was now more realistically limited as the size and shape of the items you carried had to fit in his attache case. Small items like first aid spray take up 2 spaces while weapons may occupy 10 spaces or more.

While playing, I often made difficult choices about which items I would keep with me, even using up or dropping items that were valuable, but less important.

The same is true in our own schedule. There are many times we need to say, "no" to good things so we are free to say, "yes" to great things. Sometimes we get overwhelmed with the weight of everything we are carrying and we need a break. The best defense against feeling overwhelmed is to plan out your ideal week. Here's how.

How To Create An Ideal Week

1. Determine The Things You Must Do

This includes things like:

- Sleeping

- Eating

- Bathing

And any other "-ing" that needs to happen for survival.

2. List Your Obligations

We all have obligations, and they are not always a bad thing. While responsibilities may not seem as essential as sleeping or eating, they can interrupt or even supply resources for your needs. Items like:

- Work

- Spending time with your significant other

- School

- Parenting

3. List Your Wants

Next list out the things you WANT to do. Wants include:

- Watch a movie or television

- Play video games

- Hang out with friends

- All the things important to you and you enjoy

4. Estimate Time Required

Write next to each item on your list, the approximate amount of time it will take each week. For example: I want to get 7 hours of sleep each night, so I need to budget 49 hours each week for sleeping.

5. Prioritize and Rank

At the top of your list, place all of the items from your Needs category on your blank calendar.

Next, list out your Obligations. Determine how much time you need to spend on a weekly basis, and book all of these on your calendar.

Finally, rank your Wants and with whatever time is left, fill in the blanks. Chances are, you will run out of time before you run out of Wants. Keep a list of these Wants so that when you free up extra time, you know exactly what to do with it.

6. Review

Make sure you did not leave anything off the calendar, save and reward yourself with an item from your Want list, you earned it!

Strategic thinking, planning, balance and dealing with tension are important skills to have, but there is a vital attribute required to make them work together coherently. When our rigid thoughts bump up against reality, things can get messy very quickly. The best plans get discarded when the complicated nature of what we cannot control shows up. Moments of this degree of stress require another valuable leadership skill: adaptability.

ADAPTABILITY

"We all make choices, but in the end our choices make us."

Andrew Ryan, Bioshock

I have heard everyone from parents and psychologists to presidents and celebrities recommend that when a person becomes upset, it is best to just count to 10 before moving on in a calm, collected manner. I cannot speak for you, but I have been in many situations that 10 seconds is nowhere near enough time to settle down. In fact, I think 10 days would be more appropriate.

A common feature in arcade games is a countdown timer. After you have lost a game, a 10 second countdown is displayed on screen, giving you the chance to find another quarter, insert it into the machine, and hit start to continue. The problem I faced with this screen, aside from seeing it all too often, was that it frazzled my nerves. It was an intense moment, where you shifted from concentrating all your focus on the game, to now having to fumble around to find and manipulate a quarter into the machine, while all your progress (and sometimes the fate of the world) hangs in the balance. I don't like countdowns.

The problem with both countdown scenarios, is that the emotional energy is already there. Once the emotion kicks in, our brains are working in fight or flight mode and our ability to function rationally is greatly hampered. We start processing irrational thinking:

What if I don't have any more quarters? What if it gets stuck in my pocket? What if I drop it and it rolls under the machine?

I have to continue! I cannot lose! I've just got to keep playing!

So what? It is just a game. It does not matter at all. Who cares, anyways?

How to Keep People from Mashing Your Buttons

When we think along these lines, we still have not solved the problem, and in most cases, we have either escalated the anxiety substantially, or we have completely dismissed the situation all together (also not healthy). So what does that leave us with? I would like to recommend an approach that has changed my life. In *How to Keep People from Pushing Your Buttons*, Albert Ellis, proposes Realistic Preferences.

I am a fan of all styles and genres of video games, but I really enjoy an occasional head-to-head match in a fighting game. While I am primarily a fan of the *Street Fighter* series, I also have a special place in my heart for *Tekken*. When *Tekken* first came out in arcades, it caught the attention of arcade goers in my area. I remember small crowds huddled around the game, loving the fast pace, and flashy nature of the game. I was not very good at the first game, but by the time *Tekken 3* was released, I had improved my skills considerably. I spent hours mastering moves and powerful combos and I thought I was ready to head to the arcade and take on the challengers. Except that *Tekken 3* had a bit of a problem. Experienced and inexperienced players are almost on equal ground. The game seems to be designed in such a way, that a new player who just mashes their attack buttons randomly can overcome an experienced player in a way that defies logic and all that is right in the world.

In the same way, we can find ourselves in arguments with others who seem to say random things just to upset us, meanwhile we are trying to use proper technique, explain our position and listen to theirs. So how do you overcome this situation? Sometimes, you have to just let that 10 second countdown run out and walk away. For most situations, walking away in is not the best answer, and many times, it is not an option. When dealing with the most common examples, the best approach I have found is adopting Realistic Preferences.

How Realistic Preferences Give You the Winning Edge

The mindset behind realistic preferences is acknowledging that in life, most of the things that upset us, the things that push our buttons or that can set us off course, are really just violations of our own personal preferences. When we think in absolutes about things that, "must" and "should" be, we create a line in the sand. When there is a line that is drawn, that means the line can also be crossed or broken. Sand is not the best place to draw a long lasting line anyway.

Adopting a mindset of realistic preferences is not that difficult in concept. It can be as simple as changing your vocabulary.

"I have to win." vs. "I prefer to win."

"You cannot speak to me that way." vs. "I wish you would not speak to me that way."

"I must have Chicago as my team" vs. "My first choice is Chicago."

In the first example of each pair, we see a fixed, inflexible, and unrealistic thought. While I would like to win, there may be things are outside my control. Sure, I need to do my best, but I also need to be open to the possibility it might not end up the way I want. Every time you have heard a parent tell their children "I am not going to repeat myself," what happens? The parents end up repeating themselves and are further upset because they are now a liar.

Realistic Preferences Generate Adaptability

When we adopt a realistic preference mindset, we can face the reality that while things might not go how we prefer, it is not the end of the world. This realization makes a surprising difference in our emotional investment in the outcome. It also provides the wherewithal to adapt to situations that face us. When we allow situations to push our buttons, we fix ourselves into rigid responses that inevitably lead to actions we regret. Bruce Lee said "All fixed set patterns are incapable of adaptability or pliability. The truth is outside of all fixed patterns." When others are involved, this can lead to conflict. Conflict is not absolutely bad – often it can be good, but it must be handled successfully.

Have you ever found yourself in a conversation where you and the other individual did not see eye to eye? How did it go? Chances are, not as well as you would like. Conflict in video games seems so much easier. There are rules, a third party keeps track of the score in an objective fashion, and at the end there is a clear winner. Most of us feel competent in video game conflict, but real life conflict is a messy thing.

Imagine being at work when an unexpected conflict breaks out. A life bar appears overhead, then you and your coworker are prompted by your boss: "Round One, Fight!"

A few PowerPoint slides and Excel pivot tables later, you are declared the winner. You pose dramatically in the meeting room as your theme song plays. Then everyone goes back to work, no hard feelings. In *Dead or Alive*, *Marvel vs Capcom*, and *King of the Fighters* we all have to play by the same rules. Rules are typically unbreakable, and we respect others' performance. We are all speaking the same language. Not so in the real world.

All Your What Are Belong To Who?

Part of conflict is the messy nature of Communication. There are so many variables in communication, from the environment, to the sender of the message, or the receiver of the message, a lot can go wrong. Just look at the recent announcement from CEO of Tesla Motors, Elon Musk entitled "All Our Patent Are Belong To You," referencing the classic line from the game *Zero Wing*. Gamers and those "in the know" got a laugh out of the clever "all your base" reference, but the media found themselves very confused. Individuals on Tesla's blog offered up grammatical corrections. Who doesn't love a grammar Nazi, especially when they miss the point? Successful communication and conflict resolution is a very complicated thing, but also very important.

In the life changing book *Crucial Conversations*, Patterson, Grenny, McMillan, and Switzler provide some outstanding thoughts on dealing with conflict. Let's take a look at some of the best ways for successfully approaching disagreements.

Work On Me First

I know I am guilty of saying this over and over, but "I can only control me." In multi-player video games, you control your own character, not everyone else's characters. So if I want to win, then I have to play my best and make sure I do the right things I need to do to win.   If we are to be successful in communication, we need to focus on what we can do to help the outcome. If the other person is not understanding, then I need to look at how I am speaking, and adjust accordingly.

Am I being respectful? If it is my wife, am I being loving in how I speak? How is my tone of voice? If others spoke to me the way I speak to them, how would it make me feel?

As long as we focus on other person, we will get nowhere. Even if I could change the other person, I would just run into the same communication problems with the next person I disagree with. Stephen Covey is famous for the advice: "Seek first to understand, then to be understood." Like intercepting a rocket in the game *Missile Command*, I need to know where the projectile is coming from and where it is going before I can attempt to connect with it.

Focus On What Is Really Important

Have you ever gotten distracted in a game? With larger game worlds, especially open world or sandbox style games, it can become easy to be distracted. Consider how much time you have spent fishing in any of the *Legend of Zelda* games, or how much time you lost to *Triple Triad* in *Final Fantasy VIII*. In the same way, we can easily be pulled into conflict where we miss the point of the entire conversation. When we end up in conflict, it is important to think about what we really want out of the interaction.

Ask yourself these questions:

"What do I want for myself?"

"What do I want for others?"

"What do I want for this relationship?"

Then ask yourself, "How would I behave if this was what I really wanted?"

This question will give you a lot of insight on how to get the conversation back on track. Having clear goals and reflecting on our progress towards these goals will prevent us from forgetting we still need to save the world at some point.

Mute & Berserk – How We Respond

When any of us are in a conversation where we do not feel safe, we respond in one of two ways – we either respond with Silence or with Violence. You can find a near direct parallel to the two responses in the *Final Fantasy* game series, in the form of the spells Mute or Berserk.

Mute

In *Final Fantasy*, getting hit with Mute means that a character cannot cast any spells, they have lost their voice. In real life, a response of Silence is essentially the same thing. Silence means we clam up, and we may give others the silent treatment.   We avoid conflict, and do anything we can to make the discomfort stop, avoiding dealing with the real issue, as long as the conflict ends.

Berserk

Berserk has a very different outcome in *Final Fantasy* when compared to Mute. Berserk causes the affected character to enter a state of uncontrollable rage, physically attacking every turn. In the same way, Violence means we attack the other person in the conflict, verbally and emotionally. We may become defensive and say things like "Who are you to say that?" or "You're even worse than me!" We try to dominate the other individual until the conflict is over.

Rage Quitting: Fight And Flight

In the online gaming world, we even have a balanced response that is both equal parts Violence and Silence: the Rage Quit. This happens when playing online competitive matches, often in head to head fighting games, where one player becomes so upset over the direction of the match they will forcefully quit the match, game, or even shut off their gaming console. When online matches were still perfecting their systems, the player not quitting often was robbed of a "win" or experience points by the rage quitter, but as game developers noticed this trend, adjustments have been made that will penalize the Rage Quitter.

Too bad systems like this don't exist in the real world. Imagine if we were all forced to fight fair?

But as long as we are thinking this way, we still are seeing conflict as a win/lose proposition. The thing about communication is that you need not have a winner and a loser. If you listen carefully, and look at what you can do to improve the situation, you just might find an outcome that everyone will benefit from. If you start a conversation with the assumption you are right or you must win, it is difficult to really talk.

Remember, that when you enter into a conflict, you don't have all the facts – neither side does, so it is important to be patient, listen, focus on what you can agree on, then move forward carefully.

It is not always easy, but it is always worth it.

That being said, there are still decisions and events in life that really are that important, or tied to consequences that can be life altering or even life ending. These moments often arrive in times of significant change. Change has become the new normal, with technology exponentially accelerating change. Adapting to change is not enough in the workplace of the future – one must also be able to navigate large-scale change successfully.

CHANGE MANAGEMENT

"When things fall, they fall... Life's a game of chance. You play your cards, and Fate plays hers."

Setzer Gabbiani, Final Fantasy VI

Change is the new normal in today's modern societies. The rate that change happens is staggering. Just 10 years ago you would never have considered buying a phone from a computer company or trusted the review of a total stranger to make a purchase online. Technology has a way of rapidly accelerating change in ways we have dreamed about, but also in ways we never could expect. Being able to deal with fast-paced and large scale change is a key skill for playing a leading role within a business of any kind.

The video game industry itself has undergone quite a bit of change since its inception. Even considering one aspect of video games, such as graphics, you can see tremendous progress each decade. That topic is easily another book unto itself.

As a video game enthusiast, I can honestly claim that I have saved the world many times over. Is it possible that a solution might be hidden in video games for solving large scale real world issues?

Rolling With Change

I love the *Katamari Damacy* series. It is so quirky and odd, but very accessible and fun to play. *Katamari Damacy, We Love Katamari, Me and My Katamari*, and *Katamari Forever* are all pretty much the same game. Sure you could argue the difference with me, but the core of each game is the same. The King of All Cosmos is involved with accidentally destroying all the planets and stars in the sky, and the Prince (along with his cousins) are tasked with rebuilding everything by rolling up stuff with a sticky ball called a Katamari.

That's about as good of an explanation that I can muster.

Much more important than the plot, or even the basic game mechanics is the possible lessons that this odd little game can teach us about solving something as complex and important as managing change within an organization. If you have played any of the Katamari games, you already know a lot about managing change. In fact, you have been exposed to the principles that are found in Change Management Expert John Kotter's model for change. I present to you:

Katamari Damacy And John Kotter's 8 Steps For Change

Create a Sense of Urgency

Before the Prince can roll the Katamari, he is given a little background about his mission including specific target size of the Katamari and time limit. The story for each level also includes compelling reasons for rolling up stuff, not the least of which is replacing planets and stars accidentally destroyed by the King of All Cosmos (it's a long and strange story).

When you are trying to bring about a change, there has to be a sense of urgency, otherwise there is no reason to start the change. Just as in Katamari, a time limit helps others to focus on what actions they must take and can increase their willingness to take part in new behaviors. This sense of "we HAVE to take action" is what sets the stage for the next actions.

Form The Guiding Coalition

In large organizations, having the right people on the team is very important. John Kotter points out that at least 75% of the management team of an organization must buy-in to the need for the change or else it will have limited success. This team leading the change should be a group of individuals who are influential – this does not mean they need a "leader title," but rather they are a person who others listen to. The team should also represent the larger group of people being affected by the change.

A guiding coalition is one area where *Katamari Damacy* provides a negative example. In the game, the King of All Cosmos is calling all the shots, so the Prince (or any of his cousins) have no say in how things go down. Perhaps you have been part of an organization that has a "Command and Control" approach, where the senior team makes all the decisions for the entire organization, often with no regard for how it will impact the daily work of the individuals on the front line. The danger here is a significant loss in morale and high turnover of good employees.

Create A Vision For Change

A vision leads to inspiration. During the King of All Cosmos' introduction to each level, he offers a motivational pep-talk about how he would like to see the end result of the mission. He describes with colorful language what type of outcome he would like to see from the Prince's efforts. However, you can tell by the wording of these visions that the King has been creating them with a committee of one: himself. The vision is typically self-serving or made up to suit his desires of the moment, however odd they may be.

When designing a vision for a change effort, the team leading it should work to inspire others by building a picture of a future that is better than the current state or the potential state if no change is made. At this time a strategy should be adopted for how the change should come about, based on the nature of the vision itself. The vision is the Why, the strategy is the How and What.

Communicate The Vision

As previously mentioned, the King of All Cosmos does a good job of communicating his vision at the outset of each level. Then once the level loads, the King offers a few more thoughts about how the Prince can be successful. Several times during the longer stages, the King will even interrupt the Prince to communicate additional information or reiterate his vision for the level, however silly it may be.

In many organizations, communication is a significant challenge. Often employees will say things like "well, no one told me." Of course, this is after 6 emails, large posters all over the organization, 3 staff meetings where the manager explained in detail all the facts, a printed memo that the employee signed, and various other methods of communication. That's not to say it is always the employee's fault. There are many leaders and managers in organizations that are truly terrible communicators. When the communication focuses only on what the employees need to do, but does not include any indication as to why the employees should do it, change efforts slow dramatically. If the leader does not know how to communicate the vision in a way that is inspirational, it is time to hire someone who can help.

Remove Obstacles

It is the leader's responsibility to clear the path for employees to make the change easier. In the largest Katamari levels, there are cones or other barricades that restrict the player to a specific area. Once the Katamari reaches a specific size, the King of All Cosmos removes the barrier which allows the Prince to roll into new areas and grow the size of the Katamari exponentially. If these barriers are not removed, the player's progress would plateau and most levels could never be finished.

In the same way, those who are higher in the organizational structure have the responsibility to remove the barriers that those who report to them often face. This is not optional, it is an obligation and a primary function of management to allow the organization to succeed. And yes, sometimes it costs a lot of money and has no immediate measurable return on the investment, but it is the right thing to do. Sometimes an obstacle might even be a co-worker. Leaders need to be brave enough to make the tough call, and move that individual up through counseling or out through progressive discipline.

Create Short Term Wins

Katamari is brilliantly paced. Each level is progressively larger, but later levels are often an expansion of earlier stages. The player is not tasked with rebuilding the sun right from the beginning of the game - that is saved for much later. Instead, each level includes a summary, rewards, and in game recognition to celebrate that a stage is complete.

The wise business leader will pay careful attention to this concept and find a way to celebrate little wins frequently. Nothing motivates a team like success. I have noticed that this is why gym memberships often go unused. If I saw immediate results in my abs after working out for two nights, then you know I would be there every day. But as it is, many gym memberships go unused because a lot of hard work has to happen before true results surface. Most change is like this, but the field of Organizational Development offers techniques that can identify wins in a way that taps into the psychology of employees, but more important than their head is their heart.

The things we stick with over the long haul are things we believe in. Things we feel.

Build On The Change

As previously noted, Katamari is about gradual, progressive change. To roll up a skyscraper, you must first be able to roll up trees, and before that, be able to roll up paper clips. Katamari often makes you start out small, but eventually winds up with a Katamari so large that even planets can be rolled up.

In the same way, leaders who successfully initiate change in their organization must keep the ball rolling if they hope to see continued growth. Each success increases what the organization is capable of doing and creates fantastic momentum. When you feel like a winner, you play like a winner.

Anchor The Change

For the Prince, rolling the Katamari becomes a way of life. That's just how he rolls (it took the entire chapter to get to that joke).

Katamari demonstrates Newton's First Law of Motion – "An object at rest stays at rest and an object in motion stays in motion with the same speed and in the same direction unless acted upon by an unbalanced force." Much about this principle holds true for creating significant change. There is a natural resistance to change, but it is not the change that is being resisted so much as the individuals involved resisting being changed.

In other words, the Katamari starts out at rest, and it takes quite a bit of work to get it rolling up to speed. Once the Katamari grows to a very significant size, it can be even more difficult to get it moving with any kind of velocity.

In the same way, employees can find a level of comfort in their job, and individuals can find a level of comfort in whatever bad habit they engage in. People prefer familiar things to comfortable things. People prefer comfortable things to better things. If you want to make change happen, you must find a way to make the better thing both comfortable and familiar.

Big Change Takes Time

In the early levels of Katamari, the items you pick up are tiny and the environment you roll around in may be as small as a dining room of a house. Some levels start out this small, but end up with a Katamari so large that you are rolling up cars, houses, and even entire continents. But levels this large often take a long time and a lot of effort to successfully complete. Momentum is a big differentiator, this is where the importance of "quick wins" come into play.

Managing change is a difficult, complicated, and messy thing. It is also very rewarding for those who adopt and stick with a winning strategy. I want to leave you with one more lesson about change from *Katamari Damacy*.

113

You Can Manage Change Or You Can Manage Change With Excellence

At the end of each level, the King of All Cosmos provides you with an assessment of how you performed in the level. In fact, the quality of the planet or the star you have created in the process is assessed and rated based on how you performed, depending on metrics such as size, speed, or contents of your Katamari. The King expresses his pleasure, astonishment, or if you fail, his wrath.

In the same way, we can manage change, ram the new way of doing things down other's throats and call it a day, or we can take the time to do it well. There are many things in life and business that are pass or fail, but managing change is not one of them. How well you do matters immensely to the people in the organization, the customers you serve, and the likelihood of your long term success.

Take the time to do it right.

As the King of All Cosmos said, *"Don't expect another sequel. Live in the moment. This is one of the most important lessons in life."*

Change And The Human Factor

In business, the need for handling change effectively is even more important. The reality of today's workplace is that change is constant -

change is the new normal. One doesn't have to look far to find many examples of how technology has rapidly advanced in recent years. While technological advances move at an ever increasing pace, the most important part of any change can be often overlooked.

The human factor.

One of the greatest responsibilities and challenges of modern-day managers and leaders is the need to lead, bring about, and successfully navigate change, both in the workplace and in the external environment. Change can be big and very complicated and there are many reasons it doesn't stick. Too often emphasis is placed on the structure, systems, timing, and the details of what's being changed but often overlooked is the emotional aspect. Yes, how employees feel has a lot to do with the success of any change effort.

How Video Games Can Help with Positive Change

A great example of a video game that has made a difference in player's lives can be found in a line of games by HopeLab. HopeLab, who produces the game *Re-Mission* and *Re-Mission 2*, understands the potential that video games have to help impact behavioral change through both knowledge and emotion. In a multi-site randomized controlled trial of nearly 400 young people with cancer, HopeLab's game *Re-Mission* significantly improved: Cancer related knowledge, quality of life, cancer specific self-efficacy, and medical treatment adherence.

Re-Mission 2: Nanobot's Revenge is also available on mobile devices and teaches terminology and interactive concepts in a way that is more anthropomorphic action game than the interactive edutainment titles found in classrooms. The game is free to play and I dare you not to learn something while playing. Fun game play combined with learning is just the beginning. When the learning overflows into the player's life, the real potential for video games comes into focus.

I have already addressed several of the techniques that video games use to cement learning and change behavior, but I would like to dive a little deeper into one of the most powerful techniques, one responsible for the addictive nature of many games: short term wins.

The Secret To Change That Sticks: Short-Term Wins

Another way video games can help with change efforts is the concept of generating short-term wins. As gamers, we have all experienced this idea of a short-term win. Most good games have them, either explicitly or implicitly, and place them strategically – in particular, at the beginning of the game. An excellent testament to this concept can be found anecdotally on Passive Income expert, Pat Flynn's blog post regarding his college experience with the game *World of Warcraft*. "I specifically remember the first time I played WoW, and I knew – I just knew it was going to become an addiction because during the first 10 minutes, I had already completed 2 quests, leveled up twice and unlocked several new abilities – not to mention my coin bank was already growing."

Powerful evidence of the impact of well-scripted short-term wins. So how do we harness the power of short-term wins to help us make the positive change we desire?

Let's start by taking a look at what makes for a good short-term win.

Effective Short Term Wins

1. Short-term wins need to be visible

A short term win should be verifiable, not just a rumor or hype. Exercising and diets offer few immediate signs of success. This makes sticking with the routine more difficult. Imagine if you saw dramatic results the first day you went to the gym or started that new diet – you would probably stick with it, right?

2. Short-term wins need to be clear

This win must be unambiguous, so that when many people look at it they all come to the same conclusion. This also helps with how the short-term win can be accomplished, because when there is clarity around what we are doing, how we get there is less important than why we are doing it in the first place. If we are not sure if we really achieved a win or not, then it might as well not have happened.

3. The short-term when has to be linked back to some larger change effort

If the win is completely unrelated or not useful to a larger goal/larger scale objective, then it doesn't do much good – it is just a distraction. Do you have a collection of in-game Achievements or Trophies that are totally meaningless? What does it matter if you get an award for playing 10 online matches, or advancing the story by one chapter? These awards feel arbitrary and fail to create any real results. A carefully crafted win can have the exact opposite effect.

Why Short-Term Wins Matter

There are many factors that contribute to the success of short-term wins. They provide a great source of feedback in terms of progress. Video games the break the experience up into stages, checkpoints, levels and worlds. If we didn't have a way to measure progress in video games, gaming could become tedious, exhausting, or cause us to lose interest.

There is interesting research around the chemical benefits that quick wins generate in the gaming world. Much of the research is concerned with understanding the perceived addictive nature of gaming. Results often conclude that gaming is not universally addictive, but there are elements of video game design that can be. I can tell you without digging into significant research, that winning just feels good.

A Winner Is You

The video games we love build natural breaks into the game to celebrate a victory with animation bonuses, fireworks, new items, improved skills of a character in the game, or useful rewards of some kind – all are very appealing ways to celebrate the short-term win. What *Final Fantasy* fan doesn't immediately smile when they hear the victory fanfare from the game?

Role playing video games in general offer tremendous sources of positive feedback and opportunities to celebrate short-term wins. The game system itself is typically built on experience points you earn for defeating enemies. At the beginning of most games, you start out at a low level, but the good news is that you can quickly gain experience and increase your levels in a short time from starting.

Many games scale the experience needed to level up based on your current levels or the amount of progress you have completed so far. Growing from level 1 to level 2 takes very little time when compared to moving from level 50 to level 51. Too often in the business world we set our goal to achieve level 51, only to forget about the celebration in recognition of achieving levels 1 through 50.

Most players don't meticulously track every single experience point they are earning in a role playing game, but rather show up to battle, overcome the enemy, and press forward. As long as the game system responds in a way that is fair and generally predictable, most players are not particularly concerned about the precise amount of experience points they earn for every single battle.

What happens, however, is that momentum is built. As you see levels increased and challenges overcome, you become connected to a game. You often hear gamers talk about becoming "immersed in an experience" or starting a game to play for 30 minutes, only to find out many hours later how involved they actually became.

Changing Things One Level at a Time

As leaders we can take these concepts, and if we successfully build them into any change that has to happen in the workplace, we will find those around us are both more willing to move with the change as well as more engaged in the change, possibly providing amazing ideas along the way.

This is why big companies creating large-scale change efforts encounter so much trouble – too often leaders and managers don't plan out the creation of specific short-term wins. In this way, the leader's role in any organization is a bit like the game designers' role. Change expert John Kotter offers a succinct call to action in his book *Leading Change*: "The job of management is to win in the short term while making sure you're in an even stronger position to win in the future"

It's amazing what motivational power can be unlocked with a good short-term win. Motivation is a delicate flame, capable of starting a raging fire or being blown out by the breeze while it is still small. Hope and vision are the factors that serve as oxygen and kindling for the flames of change to grow.

Solving World Hunger

What if your largest problem has already been solved? What if all you needed to do was find the person who is doing it right and make it easier for them to show others how they do it?

In the field of Organizational Development, some of the things I routinely stress about are thoughts like:

"How do we make ideas stick?"

"Once I create a training program, how do we follow up and make sure that the training is still being executed?"

"Isn't there a switch you can just flip to change your company's culture?"

I know, these are like world peace, solving poverty, or hunger issues, right?

Exactly.

That is why I am thrilled to share with you a method that just might have the answer to all the above. Well, world peace might be a stretch, but the issue of hunger or malnutrition, in this case, is not.

Enter Positive Deviance Man

Mega Man 2 is my favorite game in the Mega Man franchise, and may possibly be one of the best video games of all time. The game is pure fun, but I recall an impossibly difficult segment of the game, especially the very first time I played it as a young child. After battling eight robot masters and three stages of Dr. Wily's Castle, I found myself stuck on stage four. I even called the Nintendo hint line because I got stuck here, fighting the end boss. If you have played the game, you know exactly what I am talking about. The stage four boss is a set of mounted cannons in a room full of walls you can destroy. Walls & wall mounted cannons. Did I really need to call for help on this one? Actually, I really did need help. The cannons can only be dispatched with the Crash Bomb weapon, and the walls guarding them can only be broken by the Crash Bomb, as well. So far, so good, right?

The problem is that your weapon's use is limited, and you do not have enough to break all the walls and still blast all the cannons. Meanwhile, the cannons just keep firing away from behind their safe walls. I imagine if they had faces, they would be laughing at me as I was running around the room, out of Crash Bombs, simply delaying my inevitable death (though I did gain some good practice figuring out how to dodge their firing pattern, which helped me quite a bit in my future attempts).

I mentioned that I called the Nintendo hint line. Their solution? Blow up all the walls, die, restart the stage, refill the Crash Bomb weapon, then finish off the boss. Fine and good unless you only have one life left, or you are trying to complete the game with one life. It turns out there is another solution. A deviant one.

When I say deviant, I am defining the word as "departing from the norm," so get your mind out of the gutter. I learned a deviation from the typical approach to winning this boss battle, and it requires some strategic uses of items 1 & 3, while ignoring a few breakable walls.

Here is what I learned: You can win without dying.

Positive Deviance In Action

Back In the 1990's Jerry Sternin was part of a group called "Save the Children" that sought to help Vietnam deal with the challenge of malnutrition in children among rural villages. Jerry, his wife, and their 10 year old son made the trip to see what could be done about this issue. At the time almost 65% of the children under 5 years of age in Vietnam suffered from malnutrition to some extent. Complex political factors and governmental changes combined with devastating typhoons only made matters worse.

In addition to all these factors, Jerry was even told point blank that there were many who did not even want him in the country, and that he would only have 6 months to produce results. Since the government of the country did not have the resources needed to solve this problem, Jerry would basically need to figure out a solution from within the villages themselves. That last apparent "problem" proved to be where the answer was hidden.

Hidden In Plain Sight

When observing the families in the village, Jerry and his group of volunteers made an interesting discovery: even though almost 64% of the children were malnourished, there were children from even the poorest households who were well-nourished. If even the poorest families could overcome the problem of malnutrition, then it follows that the households who were better off could see the same results. So the big question here was "what did those well-nourished but very poor families do differently?"

In other words, what made them "Positive Deviants," that is different from the rest, in a positive way? More than just an interview was needed as those who were Positive Deviants did not even realize that they were doing something different from the rest. These families were carefully observed before, during, and after mealtimes. The differences were both minimal and significant.

The Positive Deviant families:

Fed their children the sweet potato greens that other families treated as garbage.

Fed their children little shrimp, crabs, and snails found in the rice paddies (considered inappropriate by other families).

Fed their children smaller, more frequent meals.

Once the differences were identified, a high-involvement cooking class with plenty of hands-on experience combined with some clever ways to build the habit of collecting the extra ingredients helped the solution stick. The answer was hidden in plain sight.

Positive Deviance In Your Own Stage

Now look at some of the challenges in your workplace – are there individuals who are successful in the same environment, perhaps even unaware that they are doing something differently in such a way that others could benefit? Check out the Positive Deviance Website (http://www.positivedeviance.org/) for more case studies, and great tools that you can use to apply the Positive Deviance approach to the biggest problems! I also highly recommend the *Positive Deviance Field Guide*.

Now about world peace…

MASTERING THE GAME

CLEARING THE ENTITLEMENT LEVEL

"You should have ruled this planet. You were stronger, smarter. But then they came, those inferior dullards...They came and took this planet away from you. But don't be sad, Mother. I am with you now."

Sephiroth, Final Fantasy VII

"I wish I had your problems."

Have you ever thought something like this?

Did you know that someone out there is probably thinking that very thought about you? The more we have in life, the more trivial our problems can become. To unlock our highest levels of success, we need to clear the level known as entitlement. Entitlement is dis-empowering. Like an incredibly difficult stage in a video game, failure to complete this stage and move past it will halt your progress.

My own video game parallel is the Phantom Chest in *The Legend of the Dragoon*. I was so excited to pick up this role playing game for the Playstation, and I was making great progress when I arrived at the

127

treasure chest in the Phantom Ship area of the game. For some reason, I just could not figure out this puzzle. Inside the treasure chest puzzle were random numbers that had to be entered to unlock the chest. Even the online guide I found was not helping me progress. It aggravated me to the point of tears. Eventually I just gave up and sold the game. Once my momentum died, I no longer felt like even playing the game. An attitude of entitlement in real life will do the same thing to your ability to succeed.

1st World Gamer Problems

I've got too many games, I don't know which one to play.

I master the offline mode, only to get slaughtered online.

I memorize and practice all the special moves and combos, only to get beaten by a button masher.

It seems like every time I turn on my current gen system, I have to update the firmware. Again.

After updating the system firmware, your new game requires an update. Might as well just go to bed/work/school since it won't finish until you no longer have time to play.

I actually bought a game at a yard sale that I already own – I just could not remember it was already in my collection.

Pathetic, right? My big problem and complaint for the day was that I had run out of space to display all my video games. Not exactly a bottom level need on Maslow's Hierarchy. Trust me, I checked. Nope, "lack of display shelf for Neo Geo AES cartridges" is not anywhere on that list. Never mind that I don't even have that much time to play anyways. But instead, I focus on system updates and broadband internet lag. It is almost like we are wired to look for problems.

Someone Else Would Love To Have Your Problems

I realized others wish they had my problems. How many people in this world wish they could enjoy playing a game? Any game? In his Podcast "In the loop," episode 94, Andy Andrews talks about "How to Practice Gratitude." He tells a great story about the difference between "having to" and "getting to." What does this look like for you and me?

If you have a job, you don't "have to" go to work, you "get to" go to work. Just ask someone who has been job hunting for some time how much they would like to have your problem of "having to go to work today." Too often it is easy to see something as a bother, rather than the blessing it truly is.

I am thankful for my problems. With the right mindset, I think we all can find something to be grateful for about our problems. Top executive coach Dr. Marshall Goldsmith shared a sobering experience with me during an interview I co-hosted with Jared Easley for the *Starve the Doubts* podcast:

> "I went to Africa when they had the Great Famine Campaign of 1984 and I was there for 9 days. I was there with the Red Cross and it was taped on NBC News – it was on TV every day for a week.
>
> I watched a lot of people starve to death while I was there.
>
> Now I have a picture in my library, and the picture is of me when I was back in Africa, and I am sitting next to a woman who is measuring the arms of children. She is doing this because they only fed children between the ages of 2 and 16, because they didn't have enough food. So if you are over 16 or under 2, you got to die. Otherwise she would measure your arms. If the arm was too little, she would say 'well, you're going to die anyway, go over there.' If the arm was too big, they were considered not hungry enough, and she would tell them to step out of the line.
>
> If your arm is in the middle, then you get food.
>
> So in the picture I am looking at the camera, trying to send myself a message, the me then, looking at the me

now, trying to say this: Be happy with what you have. Your kids are not in this line. You're not in this line.

Be happy, life is good."

How is that for a sobering thought to pull us back into present reality? Even with a clear mind or a heart in the right place, we still run into walls and face frustrations. The most frustrating time of all can be the in-between times. Those moments where we find ourselves waiting. Let's call these moments "life's loading screens."

What To Do During Life's Loading Screens

Do you ever find yourself waiting? If you are into video games, maybe you are waiting for the next great game to be released. As an employee, perhaps you are waiting for a promotion or if you are in the wrong job, waiting for five o' clock. Singles are often waiting to find Mr. or Ms. "Right," just as students are eagerly awaiting the completion of their degree.

Expectant parents are waiting for the baby to be born, as many family members are just waiting for their sick loved one to get better. Many are lonely and just waiting for someone to notice them. Let's face it, we are all waiting on something. In fact, gamers have been doing a significant amount of waiting ever since games were first designed. I remember plenty of waiting when a new game was being installed on the computer.

For a while, it seemed like home consoles had the advantage of speed through cartridge based games, until the CD ROM become the standard. Then console gamers were able to be equally annoyed by load times. Some games and systems were worse than others, but I remember the Neo Geo CD being among the worst violators. There is nothing quite like sixty-second load times before a battle in a fighting game, only to find yourself staring at another load screen after a thirty-second fight.

Some games are infamous for their long load times, but early into the CD ROM format, developers found clever ways of disguising load times, or at least giving players something interesting to do while they were waiting.

Some games offer interactive load screens like the "now loading" text from *Castlevania: Symphony of the Night* that you can scroll with the controller, or similar effects in games like *Katamari Forever* or *Noby Noby Boy*. The original *Tekken* on the Playstation even featured the bonus level for Galaga as a playable mini game during the initial load screen (that is when you know your load times are bad).

The bottom line: Waiting is inevitable. What you do while you wait is the important part. Let's take a look at a couple of typical responses we can have to waiting: Impatience, Indifference, or Initiating Action.

Impatience

Impatience can lead to anger. Anger leads to hate. Hate leads to suffering. Next thing you know, you are a sith lord that sounds asthmatic. Dangerous stuff. I have seen far too many gamers angered by excessive load times or barriers that exist in a game that prevent progress.

I think back to the first *Sonic the Hedgehog* game on the Sega Genesis. If you left Sonic standing still for more than a few seconds, he began tapping his foot waiting for you to input a command. Seriously, even the video game is getting impatient now. Impatience can come at a high cost. In video games, we lose our lives, resources, and even in game progress to impatience. In real life, the stakes are even higher.

Not waiting can kill a career, a relationship, or even put your life at risk. Almost a decade ago, my impatience while driving resulted in my car being totaled, and could have resulted in serious injury.

Indifference

Indifference in many ways is the opposite of anger. Waiting can drain our energy, and even our passion. It may result in us developing a careless attitude, which can also have profound consequences. When we disengage, we don't play our best, our work is subpar, and our relationships are slowly bled dry.

Indifference is more dangerous than impatience in some regards, since it is deceptive and leads to a demotivated state that can greatly impact our overall well-being. Think back to a time when you were playing a video game and realized that you did not even care about it. You were just wasting time, lives, in-game resources, you name it - the game became a burden, or even felt like work. When we get disconnected to our "why" this is what happens.

Initiating Action

The third response to waiting falls into the difficult balance between impatience and indifference. I like to refer to this mindset as adopting a realistic preference. We identify what we prefer as an outcome, but are also brutally honest with ourselves, that reality might just take a bit longer than we wish. When we take this stance, we can then ask ourselves really good questions like "What can I do while I am waiting?"

What To Do While You Wait

Grind for Money and Rare Drops

I mean this in the literal since. Let's say you are waiting for a promotion or to end up with the perfect employer. If you are looking to increase your available cash, there are really only two ways to do this: Increase your income or Decrease your spending.

Now I know that is pretty darn obvious, but let's look at a couple ways we can do both. When it comes to increasing your income, you can look for the perfect job or wait on the promotion, but if we are looking to initiative action, then what else can we do?

We can get a 2nd job, maybe something part time. That will increase your income in the short run. You can also start up your own business. I promise it is not as difficult as it sounds. Sell things on eBay, craigslist, or etsy – it has never been easier for anyone with a computer to make money.

What about decreasing your spending? Well, the best way to do that is to make sure you have an accurate budget, and stick closely to it. My wife and I found almost $300 a month we were spending on eating out and other little things. What would you do with another $300 a month? You could pay off a car, a student loan, or make extra payments on the mortgage. I can't tell you how good it feels to have no monthly car payment!

And yes, my home is completely paid off too (in *Animal Crossing*, not real life. Yet.).

Level Up

In almost every RPG, winning a victory over the enemy gives you "stuff." This stuff can be money and rare drops, like we just discussed, but there is also another benefit from winning battles: Experience. In fact, many games allow you to fight the same enemies over and over so that a patient player can level up their characters in such a way that they have a strong advantage over upcoming challenges.

In the *Final Fantasy* series (VI & VII especially) I found myself doing a fair amount of leveling up. I enjoy putting the time in up front so that later on I can overcome difficulties at a much faster rate. One of the most demotivating things for me personally, is to rush ahead only to get stuck against a boss I am too weak to defeat.

So while you are waiting, how can you build skills? Take a look at your job today – is there something more you can do to help you learn a new skill? What about checking out a book on personal development, or taking some classes for a certification in your desired field? These are all great ways to take advantage of resources you might have available, because later on, you will be glad you did.

Support Others

Maybe you feel like you are doing everything you can to develop yourself, and take advantage of the position you are in whole you are waiting, but what about those around you? How can you help them, or even teach them about things you know? Rarely, if ever, have I truly regretted supporting others. It is easy to tear others down, to criticize what they are doing. Supporting and recognizing others can go a long way.

There Will Always Be Load Times

It is important to slow down and observe the world around us – we can't all be like Kirby, just inhaling everything in sight without even chewing. As technology advances, so does the potential complexity – for this reason, load screens are here to stay. While waiting in life, and even video games, is unavoidable, it does not have to be wasteful.

So how does one move past entitlement and waiting to self-awareness and gratitude so they can take action and save the world? It's not very sexy, but it is effective: personal accountability.

PERSONAL ACCOUNTABILITY

"Your enemy is the old you! The new you will get a little bit faster every day until you're the best around!"

Rudy, Animal Crossing New Leaf

Ignorance can be frustrating. What you don't know can kill you. I don't mind saying I am ignorant, of many things. I even choose to be ignorant of information - we all do. Choosing ignorance is a matter of necessity when you consider all there is to know. For example, I choose to be ignorant of the vast majority of sports video games. That is not to say that sports games are all terrible or a waste of time, but I have placed a much lower value on them as it relates to what is important to me. I have to start by acknowledging that this ignorance is a choice.

Sometimes the knowledge we choose to be ignorant of is unimportant, like the example of a specific genre of video game. Other times this choice can be career or life limiting. We can see the consequences played out in a safe way within video games, and apply what we learn to our own lives.

Start With Yourself

Almost every video game can demonstrate the principle of personal accountability in any number of ways. I think of all arcade platformers as being epically guilty of this, but a measure of this is intentional. Arcade machines are driven by their ability to surprise the player with new challenges, often forcing them to learn their lessons the hard way as they go along. After all, if you were warned about every possible challenge in the game before facing it, you would not need to continue as much. An arcade machine that takes one of your quarters or tokens for an hour of play time is not a good business model.

Sometimes lessons are learned the hard way. Screenwriter and voice actor for the charter Solid Snake from the *Metal Gear Solid* series, David Hayter told me about that a lesson he learned from the game *Oddworld: Abe's Odessy.* "You want to be right up to the ledge before you jump, or you will be destroyed by some horrible mutant crab creature." He's right, you know.

Here are a few examples that have taught me a thing or two about this idea of "what you don't know, can still kill you."

Given the Bird

Ninja Gaiden for the Nintendo Entertainment System (NES) is a well-loved classic, famous for having story telling cut scenes, an awesome soundtrack, and a difficulty level that borders on tear inducing. As a side note, the arcade game of the same name is a completely different game, leading to a bit of a bait-and-switch scenario to a young impressionable gamer.

While I appreciate that hardware limitations of the time played a large role in this situation, there are a number of other games released during the 80's and 90's that shared little more than a name with an arcade counterpart. I managed to be let down by *Strider, Teenage Mutant Ninja Turtles* (later corrected with *TMNT: The Arcade Game*), *Double Dragon, Bad Dudes,* and *Bionic Commando,* just to name a few home of the games that differed completely from the arcade counterparts. But I digress.

In *Ninja Gaiden* for the NES, you are a ninja, hopping around and killing bad guys, panthers, and mythical samurai, when suddenly you are introduced to a powerful force of evil in the form of…

A bird.

Not a monster sized beast, but a bird with normal powers, save for the thirst it has for dive bombing skilled ninjas. All my skills were rendered useless when this crazed *bird* flies out of nowhere and performs a mid-air takedown on me. Now the invincible ninja is falling down a bottomless pit, thanks to a small bird.

"Why didn't someone tell me? I didn't know a bird could do THAT…"

Many times, my inability to avoid connecting with the flying animal wildlife directly led to the outcome of staring at a game over screen. I guess another important lesson to take away would be if you are looking to protect your house from ninjas, skip the attack dogs or hired bodyguards. Instead invest in a few birds and use the money you saved to take a long vacation.

I Had A Good Head On My Shoulders

1998, July. Raccoon City. You are a well-trained member of an elite Special Forces team, versed in Special Tactics And Rescue Services. You are investigating the site of where your compatriots, Bravo Team, went missing. Without warning you are attached by a dangerous creature and you flee into a nearby mansion. Once inside the mansion, another member of your team goes missing. Things go from strange to outright bizarre when you encounter a zombie capable of absorbing almost all of your ammunition before dropping to the ground, seemingly dead.

I don't think I have ever been as scared while playing a video game as when I first experienced *Resident Evil* on the Sony Playstation in 1996. I was playing the game with a friend who had just purchased the new gaming console, and neither of us knew what to expect from the experience. At the time, the graphics looked amazing, and combined with the high quality music and live action introduction, I experienced an emotion that I never had while playing any game previously: fear.

To make matters worse, my friend did not have a memory card for the Playstation and as a result we were unable to save our progress, so death meant starting completely over. That did not stop us from staying up all night, just to see how far we could go in the game. A week later I purchased the game for myself, even before owning a Sony Playstation.

I soon found myself progressing through the game, enjoying the surprises that continued to unfold along the way. Walking the dangerous halls of an abandoned mansion, creeping with slow moving zombies, when I encounter what looked like a cross between a gorilla and an alligator. Next thing I knew, it is lunging at me, clawed arm extended. I held my ground, bracing for the hit, ready to unload a clip into the creature, only to realize that my head is no longer attached to my body.

I also realize that I don't have a recent save file.

"Someone should have warned me! One hit? Really?!"

One touch spikes. Harmless looking mushrooms. Water. Fire. Flying Happy faces. Electrical Seaweed. Any number of innocent or random things can end a game with precious little warning.

But this principle applies to our lives as well.

142

Squirrels Die Too

Back around 2001, I was working at the Chesterfield hotel in Palm Beach Florida – it was a great place to work, with an awesome team of professionals. (That was the most emotional job for me to leave – the people treated each other like family.) One thing about South Florida, is that you have the always present squirrel running around. Palm Beach Island, for all its greatness, still has a squirrel or two. They can often be seen darting back and forth through the streets, causing panic in drivers everywhere. They also like to climb around on power lines, usually with a higher degree of success than their street crossing efforts.

Usually.

One day while working at the front desk of the hotel, I heard a loud bang, like gunfire, and suddenly, the electricity to the building cut off. For a little while, we had no idea what happened. One valet called me over to see something he found. There in the grass, just below the telephone pole that carries the power lines, was a crispy, fried squirrel. I mean, really crispy. Apparently, the squirrel misjudged a jump, or bit a wire, and was electrocuted.

Intent And Ignorance Is Irrelevant

When things go wrong, we can ask ourselves bad questions. Questions that often lead to blame and finger pointing, but seldom change the outcome. Just because we don't know the dangers involved, does not mean we are spared from the consequences of our choices.

It is like that conversation with the police officer who pulls a guy over for speeding. "I am sorry officer, I had no idea it was only 45mph on this road." Ignorance of the law is no excuse, right? There are still consequences, but it is nothing personal.

In cases where we find ourselves facing undesirable consequences of our actions (or inaction), we often resort to defending our intentions. This concept is described by Organizational Health expert, Patrick Lencioni in his book *the Advantage*.

The Fundamental Attribution Error

This is our tendency to view other's mistakes as an extension of their personality and we judge them by their behaviors. Indeed, we even use their behavior to identify what we believe their intentions and motivations are.

However, when it comes to examining ourselves, we consider our internal intentions and motives as overriding factors, even to the point of dismissing our actions and behaviors, saying "that's not what I meant" or we tell others "you are misinterpreting my actions." This also leads us to be much more lenient on ourselves, while exhibiting a significantly harsher view of others.

This phenomenon is often apparent in head to head competitive games, where a win or loss is at risk, but even more importantly, the respect of other players. I can't begin to count the number of times that the controller, internet connection, or any other number of factors were cited as the cause for a loss in this environment. Perhaps you have been the winner, only to have your rival explain that you never would have won if they had a joystick that was not stuck, or if your internet connection was not lagging.

When others give us excuses like this, the most common reply is "yeah right, sure it was the controller." Ironically, we have no trouble finding very similar reasons to defend our losses, with one of my most popular favorites being "you just got lucky this time, that's all."

Turning The Tables

Personal growth is inherently a self-centered process. While it may deal with how we interact with or respond to others, its drive and work happens internally, and on a deeply personal level. When we read about ideas like the Fundamental Attribution Error, a natural tendency is to think about the times that others have misjudged us rather than think about the times we have misjudged them. While reading this chapter, did any names come to mind who would benefit from learning these ideas? Here is the problem: it is not our place to "fix" anyone, except for ourselves.

Be Good Enough To Beat Your Opponent And The Lag

The idea of "I can only change myself" is really important to understand. Author John G. Miller talks about the three people his father (head wrestling coach at Cornell University) reminded him that he needed to beat every time he stepped into the ring to wrestle: his opponent, himself, and the referee. He explains in his book QBQ! *The Question Behind the Question*:

> "That I had to beat my opponent was obvious. By 'myself' he meant I had to overcome the fears any athlete naturally has. About beating the ref, he'd say, 'It doesn't matter how close the match is, John. Even if you lose in overtime by one point, even if he makes a couple of questionable calls, you cannot blame the man in black and white.' He'd conclude by saying, 'If you want to win, you must be good enough to beat the ref!'"

That sounds like a tall order! Consider for a moment an individual honored in the textbooks of history. Examine why individuals are awarded medals. Think about any statue of a person you have seen. These individuals who are recognized and remember as examples to aspire to all faced adversity.

Recognition has meaning when it is earned in the most difficult of times, or even because of the difficulty in attempting something that mattered.

Florence Nightingale famously said: "I attribute my success to this - I never gave or took any excuse." In the gaming world, no one really accepts the excuses offered by a losing player. In fact, it only increases the ridicule and taunting.

The professional world is no different. No one is really interested in excuses, only results. Intentions don't matter as much as where we end up. While it may sound harsh, consider what happens in a video game when you "intend to jump" but never hit the button before you go sailing off into a bottomless pit. Intentions do not insulate us from the consequences of our actions.

Many bosses and customers have no interest in hearing about why results are not delivered as expected. I even worked for a boss who would interrupt my attempts at explanation by interjecting: "I am not looking to discuss this, I just need it done." Right or wrong, at least it was honest. There is a careful balance between understanding why a mistake happened and moving to action to correct the mistake.

Personal Accountability

Here is where all of us can step up to the plate and practice personal accountability. It can be easy to shrug our shoulders and say, "I didn't know," or come up with all the possible explanations to justify our shortcomings, but these responses are irrelevant and don't change the outcome. The same goes for the squirrel crossing the power lines: maybe he knew the consequences, maybe he did not. Either way, not knowing did not save him from the natural, immediate, and fatal consequences.

Better Questions Lead To Better Answers

In the book *QBQ! The Question Behind the Question*, John G. Miller provides a simple, yet elegant approach to creating better questions; and better questions lead to better answers.

Here is a crash course on asking better questions, using the QBQ! Approach.

1. Ask a question that starts with the word "What" or "How" (avoid using "why" or "when" or "who").

2. Use the personal pronoun "I" (not them, they, [insert other person's name]).

3. Focus on a specific action.

While it sounds incredibly simple, it is not the default approach of many individuals. For quite some time I struggled with poor questions and thought processes that led me into a frustrating place. If you are facing challenges or are unhappy about a situation in your life, asking yourself a better question can completely turn the situation around. When I stopped blaming others for situations I faced, I found that I freed up more energy and focus into accomplishing goals that had remained in limbo for the longest time.

Here are two examples of how I restructure my questions:

Before:

"When is someone going to offer me a better job?"

After:

"How can I make myself more promotable?"

Before:

"Why don't we have more resources to get the job done?"

After:

"What can I do to get the job done with what I have in front of me?"

See the difference? While subtle in structure, it is life changing in practice. Ask yourself better questions. It works because you focus on what you can do, not on what you think is out of your control. After all, I can only control me and my actions. Life is a lot better when I focus on what I can do, rather than focus on what I cannot do.

Laser Beams Can't Stop Me

Ironically, I have been practicing this thought process in video games for years. When I am playing a game and I get stuck with a puzzle or difficult boss fight, I start looking for ways that I can overcome the problem. I remember a very early breakthrough for me happened while playing *Mega Man 2* on the NES. In the Quick Man stage of the game, the player faces the infamous laser beam gauntlet. In this segment, Mega Man must navigate a series of screens where there are only moments to dodge the lasers to advance or face immediate destruction. Each time I lost a life, I would run back into the challenge, trying to figure out how I could overcome this obstacle. I did not blame the game, its designers, the President of the United States, my parents, or even the publisher, Capcom. Instead, I took responsibility for my own actions, problem solving approach, and outcomes.

I can only speak for myself here, but sometimes in life, I do the equivalent of setting down the controller or blaming bad game design on my inability to advance. In *Mega Man 2*, I discovered a weapon from another stage could freeze time, allowing me to move through the difficult segments of the Quick Man stage. Through practice, the scientific method, and memorization, I later discovered that I could complete the stage through quick reflexes and precise positioning.

Rather than asking "why can't I do this?" I asked myself "how can I do this?" This is just one more area that video game players have developed a skill that has amazing real word application, as long as we are brave enough to put it into action. While the specific techniques for managing change are numerous, none of them will be effective without a clear understanding of personal accountability.

Leveraging skills like personal accountability will earn the respect of others, both on a personal level, and eventually on the whole for the leaders of the future (and today).

How Gamers Can Get The Respect They Deserve

The gaming community seems to have a respect issue. Within the video game industry there is a lot of fighting for respect. Independent developers are fighting for the respect they deserve, musicians composing amazing scores are fighting for game soundtracks to be respected, and women are fighting for respectful depictions of their gender in games. Even gaming itself has been fighting for the right to be seen as a legitimate art form.

So the following question almost answers itself: Have you ever felt disrespected? I know I have. Do you ever feel like you are not respected in the way that you deserve? I've been there too. So how does one guarantee they get the respect they deserve?

You can't.

But if you really want to know how to improve your chances, you have to show others the respect you would like to receive.

What Respect Looks Like

We all know how it feels to be disrespected, but what does respect look like? From Barbara Glanz's *Care Packages for the Workplace: Dozens of Little Things You Can Do To Regenerate Spirit At Work* here are 5 expectations you can meet to promote a feeling of respect.

1. Listen without judging

2. Acknowledge others' differences without placing blame

3. Give others credit for their special and unique qualities

4. Assume others have a positive intention for what they do (even if how they do it does not come out right)

5. Tell the truth, with compassion when the news is difficult

If you think about a time you felt disrespected, chances are one of the 5 expectations in the list above were violated. This is where the button pushing kicks in. Once we have created an absolute way of thinking in our mind, we establish feeling associated with the violation of it. So when others judge us or fail to listen, we automatically interpret this action (or inaction) as a direct affront to who we are.

Respect is all about valuing others for who they are, and you will always be a better person for respecting others. Remember the Fundamental Attribution Error? That tendency or habit plays a large role in our disrespectful actions or words towards others. Until we can see past our own (possibly erroneous) perspective, we cannot effectively show others respect. As long as I am thinking about myself, and the respect I think I am entitled to – *I miss the point.*

I need to ask a better question of myself, knowing that better questions lead to better answers. This is where John Miller's QBQ becomes effective. I know it means we are taking more than our fair share of responsibility, but I ask "so what?" History remembers individuals who overcame resistance and those who succeed with odds against them. We build statues and memorials to the men and women who dared to challenge insurmountable odds for the sake of the greater good.

So the answer to increasing respect within and throughout the gaming community is the same answer to increasing respect in our communities and homes. We must lead by example. We must show others how it is done, to first seek to understand their needs before we try to have our own met. Anything else falls short.

In the end, it is not about getting the respect I deserve, but rather, asking how I can show others the respect they deserve. An environment of respect creates a place of safety, which in turn, sets the stage for innovation.

INNOVATION

"Maybe we'd fall short. Maybe we'd never even come close. But someone, someday, would know we'd tried."

~ Vanille, Final Fantasy XIII

Innovation is a difficult thing. All of us have been innovative at some point in our lives, but when we try too hard to be innovative it usually leads to failure. Not all innovation is good or successful, either. The video game industry is filled examples of innovation as any newly born industry will be. Some are amazing, such as 3D graphics and have changed the industry for the better. Others, like paid DownLoadable Content (DLC) have changed the industry for the worse. While it is not always apparent when innovation is good or bad, video games do provide insights into what we should learn about innovation.

Why You Should Be A Freak Like Tempest

As an arcade game, *Tempest* was a bit of a freak. It was among the very first in the market to use vector displays for the graphics, creating a very distinct, futuristic look. The graphics appear as bright glowing wireframes on a black background, with the playing field appearing as a closed tunnel or a plane with borders on either side. The player is a

"C" shaped ship that can travel only along the edge of the playing field, firing shots downward at advancing enemies.

Tempest included a level select option of sorts when continuing, allowing the player to select from various start points based on how far they advanced in the earlier game, adding difficulty selection as a unique feature.

The control scheme was a spinner knob with buttons on the left hand side, proper for the game play design of *Tempest*, but not the most common of control configurations. Uncommon control schemes are risky since you can intimate potential players from trying out the game.

Tempest also supported a progressive stage approach where the stage shape and layout changed as you progressed, with the level taking a wide range of different geometric layouts. This approach was quite different from the standard arrangement of the time, with games like *Pac Man* and *Space Invaders* keeping the same basic layouts for each stage and simply increasing speed.

The result was a very popular and desirable arcade game for players and collectors both, ranking as the 10th most popular game on the International Arcade Museum's KLOV list. Not too bad for being such a freak.

It's Good to be a Freak

Is it good to be a freak? CEO of Owner Media Group, Chris Brogan thinks so. Let me explain. Have you ever felt like you just didn't quite fit in? Do you like to approach things in a way that seems slightly different, or even contrary to the routine, safe, bland 9-5 day job? Do you know you have more to offer, but are not sure where to go next? In his work *The Freaks Shall Inherit The Earth,* Chris offers inspired advice for those of us who want to do something different: "The future is what I create today. Every day."

Freaks stay true to who they are. Freaks ask "How do I be me, more of me than anyone else can ever be? And how can I be 100% true to who I am while benefiting others?"

World Dominators Feel Fear Too

Perhaps you wish you could turn your passion into a business, or at least get paid to do what you love all day long, but maybe you think it is too strange. Maybe it's too "out there."

May I remind you that you are reading a book from a guy that is uniting video games with life and leadership lessons? I know. The fear is there. It can be overwhelming. But you can redirect it. Because it never really goes away. But it can be ignored. Then you are free to be awesome, in the way that only you can.

157

The Sequel And Another Freak

Jeff Minter is an individual who has forged a path and remained true to himself.

In 1994 he produced *Tempest 2000*, the sequel to (you guessed it) *Tempest* (see what they did there?). The game was originally released on the Atari Jaguar – the first 64bit system, leading the console wars with a claim to the most power.

Games like *Alien vs. Predator* and *Rayman* set graphical standards high at a time when the Sega Saturn and Sony Playstation were also producing increasingly realistic graphics. Yet one of the very best games is simply an update of a game from 1980, now with a fun techno soundtrack.

Tempest 2000 was a freak, and I still love it to this day.

Freaked Out Yet?

Are you dissatisfied with how things are? Do you think you know a better way, a way that things could be better? Then stay outside the box.

Feel free to eat the box if you are into that sort of thing.

Innovation often comes with the cost of being labeled a freak, enjoy the label, it means you doing something.

The Other Side Of Innovation

Innovation is often spoken of as a desired trait of leaders, and a vital skill for the next generation to possess. However, innovation is overrated. True successful innovation is rare and is often a failure. While failure can be a learning experience, innovation for innovation's sake is not efficient and not effective. More important than innovation, is knowing one's purpose. I suppose that makes this chapter a bit of a bait-and-switch maneuver, but I suspect you will be better off for it.

Part of being able to stand up and make a difference is knowing who we are. This is both simple, and incredibly difficult. Perhaps it is the largest challenge that we face, but learning who we are is also the most rewarding endeavor. Even the greatest individuals experience times where the business of life, competing demands, or unexpected events can lead to a sense of fogginess or loss of self-identity.

Our dreams are forgotten, we discard possible careers, and we find that who we are is not who we expected we would be. Some might say this is just real life setting in.

This feeling's strongest form, amnesia, is often used as a plot device in many movies and video games as well. There is something frightening, but also relatable about losing our own identity. While many of us are familiar with this plot device, thankfully few of us have experienced this

159

type of trauma to its full extent. However, there are times that all of us – myself included – have felt disconnected from our real self.

Running Through the Streets of Silent Hill

In the survival horror series, *Silent Hill,* many of the game's areas are fog enshrouded environments where seeing more than 10 feet in front of you is difficult. This makes finding buildings and landmarks a real challenge. Compounding the sense of danger is the knowledge "something" is out there, just waiting for you to take a wrong step.

There are times where we might experience our own sense of fogginess - a vague sense of confusion or disorientation, like we are running through the streets of *Silent Hill.* Other times it is just a sense of forgetting who we are, and what we are all about. When we get in a funk like this, it can be difficult to focus, concentrate, or even feel present and in the moment. It is not quite full blown depression, but it is a sense of disconnection and losing touch. The good news, is that there is hope.

Feeling Cloudy

In *Final Fantasy VII,* protagonist Cloud Strife experiences an extreme case of identity crisis, complicated by mixed memories, poor self-image, a series of laboratory experiments, followed up by a bath in the concentrated life-force of the planet.

That's pretty rough.

In the prequel, *Final Fantasy VII: Crisis Core*, we learn that Cloud's ambitions of achieving a high rank in the military were not enough to overcome his limitations, leaving him in the role of doing a lot of grunt work. He ended up settling for what he thought was the best offer at the time, hoping that someday his situation would improve. Ever find yourself working in a J.O.B. that you hate? I've been there, too.

On a military mission near his hometown, Cloud is befriended by a true Soldier First-Class, Zack, who shares many stories and experiences with him. We all need mentors, and in this case, Zack was more than just a mentor to Cloud. He was a true friend. Beyond teaching Cloud fighting techniques and skills, he also taught Cloud what it means to be a hero. Most importantly, much of his teaching was through his actions, not just lectures.

After enduring incredible obstacles and opposition, Cloud and Zack are cornered by the entire military. Realizing that he is the true target, Zack turns to face the army, but only after hiding Cloud. Zack is killed, but Cloud vows to keep his legacy alive, and essentially creates a new identity for himself combining the stories and identity of Zack with his own.

Jump forward a few years to the events of *Final Fantasy VII*. Cloud has been operating in his new identity for a while now, fooling others, but always knowing inside that something is not 100% completely right. As is the case with most epic adventure stories, extreme events happen which lead up to a comatose Cloud falling into the Lifestream (literally, the life force of the planet – think lava but less burn-up-y).

Various plot devices permit another character to enter Cloud's subconscious and work through a series of interactions to help Cloud find his true identity and shut out these false ideas and memories from his mind. The antagonist of the game (depending on your perspective) Sephiroth contributes to Cloud's loss of identity, through suggestions that his memories and identity are not reliable. He goes as far to suggest that Cloud is a fake and not capable of great things.

In the same way many of us have heard voices and thoughts that are not true but can influence us into believing lies about ourselves, who we are, and what we're capable of doing. This type of self-talk can be the source of some of our greatest limitations. I have let these kinds of voices keep me from doing great things. Maybe you have too.

How To Find Yourself Again

So what do you do if you don't have a fellow party member who can enter your mind through a stream of the planet's life-energy? How can you reconnect with your identity and who you are (or remember yourself being)?

Here is one way:

Grab a few sheets of paper and a pen or pencil and find somewhere quiet where you can be alone with your thoughts. Start by asking yourself the question:

When is the last time that I felt completely myself?

You may have to go back a long time, or it may be only a few days ago. Quickly write down a short description of that moment.

Next, with that situation clearly in your mind, consider the following questions, and write down your answers:

What

What were you doing at that moment? What about the moment made it special? What were the results of the situation? What else was happening in your life at that moment?

When

What time of the day was this? Was there a particular day of the week that contributed to the outcome? Was there a certain time of year that you felt this way?

Where

Where were you physically located? Work, school, home, at the Gold Saucer Amusement park? What was the environment like?

Who

Who were you with? Were you alone or with another individual, or perhaps a group of individuals? Were you with friends, family, or strangers?

How

How did this situation contribute to you feeling like yourself? What about the "What, When, Where, Who, and How" made the largest difference?

Take some time to reflect on the ingredients that worked together to produce that feeling of being your very best, chances are you were operating in your strengths.

Review the list you just created – what one or two answers on this list makes the biggest difference? When I did this myself, I noticed that I loved spending time alone while being creative or doing artwork of some kind. Once I identified this location and activity, I set aside time during the week to spend alone being creative.

What a difference this made! I never would have imagined something so simple could make such a difference in how I feel, but the results were almost immediate. In fact, I feel better just talking about the situation.

Self-awareness allows us to operate in our strengths, setting the stage for us to be truly excellent.

STRENGTHS

"Every hero has a weakness."

Dante, Devil May Cry

"Whether you are reckless or brave, choose the style that suits you best."

Ken, Street Fighter III 3ʳᵈ Strike

In the area of personal development, there are two prominent schools of thought – put simply, you can either work on your areas of weakness to become well-rounded, or work on your areas of strength and become exceptional in one area while remaining weak in others.

The approach I recommend can be spoiled by reading the title of this chapter. In the strengths-based approach, each person's area of greatest potential for growth can be found in her strength zone. This means that she will be best served by focusing on developing her area of greatest strength, matching the strength to her role at work, and find profound enjoyment through leveraging her greatest talents.

In *Now, Discover Your Strengths*, Marcus Buckingham and Donald Clifton make a compelling case to change our entire approach to dealing with weaknesses: "Our research into human strengths does not support the extreme, and extremely misleading, assertion that 'you can play any role you set your mind to,' but it does lead us to this truth: Whatever you set your mind to, you will be most successful when you craft your role to play to your signature talents most of the time."

Said another way, we spend far too much time on dealing with our weaknesses and trying to improve, when we are better off recognizing our strengths and working to make the most of them.

You Must Defeat Shen Long To Stand A Chance

I am a long-time fan of the *Street Fighter* series. I remember the excitement of my 14th birthday party when I took a group of friends to the local arcade just to play *Street Fighter II*. There was something exciting about the energy level surrounding the *Street Fighter II* arcade cabinet. I was amazed by the incredible graphics, intense sound, and overwhelming six button layout. Compared to other video games of the time, the roster of 8 playable characters seemed overwhelming, and I was not even sure who to select.

Over the years, with dedication and practice, my skills increased, and I was able to beat most of my friends at the game, with almost any character. Which was unfortunate, because this resulted in my friends not wanting to play against me anymore, often suggesting that we play another game instead. While many of my friends moved on to play games like *Mortal Kombat* and *Killer Instinct*, I still enjoyed playing *Street Fighter II* (plus all its iterations) and continued to work at perfecting my skills in this game.

Reliving The Past

Fast forward a decade or two to the release of *Street Fighter IV*. Obviously, I had to pick up a copy of the game for my Playstation 3. This game brought back a bunch of great memories, and along with it, the excitement and fun of playing the original. I really enjoyed this experience but the best part of all was the online head-to-head feature. Finally, I could find competitive play against others who enjoyed the game as much as I did. I also found out very quickly that I am a lot closer to the middle tier level in skill, than at the top - I guess my friends were not as competitive as I thought. And neither am I.

Ultra Street Fighter IV has a huge roster, tipping the scales at 44 selectable characters to choose for your battle. This large number of different characters all play with a wide range of fighting styles and subtle nuances, requiring significant time to fully understand. Every player and character has the ability to be competitive – there is no one player that completely outranks the others in the hands of the right person.

To be most successful in this game I have learned you need to play to your character's strengths. Once you know the style that best suits your character of choice, focus on improving their specific style of gameplay around their strengths rather than trying to play to their weaknesses. For example, if you try to play a game of speed using Zangief, the gigantic, lumbering Russian wrestler, you will be in for a hard time – trust me, it won't end well for you.

Other characters work best when played aggressively or in a defensive style. Consider the slow moving Yoga master Dhalsim. His strength lies in playing a ranging game, keeping his opponent from getting close and chipping away at their energy with various distance techniques.

Now of course there are different styles you can play while using the same character. My character of choice is the military man Guile, and for the longest time I played him with a defensive style. It seems to make natural sense, given his special moves are executed using charge commands. Charge commands require the player to hold the joystick in a specific direction for almost 2 seconds, so by default you spend a lot of time holding away, down, or even down-away while preparing for your next move.

In recent years, and especially in *Super Street Fighter IV*, I have found myself playing a much more aggressive approach using Guile. Perhaps this strategy is successful because many players expect him to be more defensive, but I discovered a lot of strong moves, techniques and strategies to use when playing a much more aggressive game. Our own strengths can also be leveraged in many different ways.

Testing Our Strengths In Battle

All of us have skills and abilities we are passionate about, and when you combine passion with a high level of skill you can find the core of your true strengths. To gain a clear picture of your own strengths, I strongly recommend the *StrengthsFinder 2.0* assessment which can be found in the book of the same name. A less precise way of identifying strengths would be to ask yourself "what am I good at that I also I enjoy doing?"

Now you can spend a lot of time trying to overcome your weaknesses but the truth is, that time will not provide a strong return on investment. Instead, the same time can be spent to become exceptional in your unique area of strengths. When I asked John Saddington, partner at the Iron Yard about an idea that has changed his life, he provided a fantastic first-hand account of what this approach looks like in action:

> "One idea that has fundamentally changed my life is when I realized that I didn't have to be good at everything. Now, it seems like such a simple truth and appears on the surface level as something very obvious. But you begin to notice when you meet with others, especially as you work into your vocation and your job,

that although many people might agree, they don't actually live this out or practice it in any way, shape or form.

There exists this pressure to do everything with excellence, to do everything well. And if you don't, then you are a failure – you're not good. We operate with a societal pressure that everything you attempt, you should be pretty good at.

We are taught this perspective at a very young age, as we work through our academic environment, we're told that we have to be good at everything. We have to be good at social studies, math, the sciences, history, and languages. Without A's in all those classes, you cannot get into a very good college, or be accepted at a top tier University. And on top of that, we must have extracurricular activities, volunteer work, and four years at the varsity level on one of the sports teams.

So we're taught at a very young age that we have to be good at everything.

But it was only after many years of doing that, and even working into my career post college, that I realized very slowly, that I did not have to be as good at everything – and there are only a few things that I was actually very good at. Even now, it feels like every year I refine that approach. I pare it down even more.

As a result, the amount of things that I am even remotely decent at becomes very, very small. What happens when this perspective has arisen in you, is that it releases you of the pressure of so much. It releases you of the pressure to try and be the best at everything. It gives you the freedom to really execute in the ways that are most natural, in the things that you are really good with. It gives you the opportunity to invest strategically in those things. Which means you get better, and become really good at those few things.

The world is in desperate need of these types of people. The world does not need more generalists, it needs more specialists. In other words: people with a very unique skill set, not more people who are mediocre at many things.

So I decided, that I wanted to become a person of exception, instead of a person of average ability in all things. And that changed my life. It helped me focus on the few things that I do well, and as a result it helped accelerate my career. It's continued to guide my decision making when it comes to career decisions. And the people I meet with, and relate with, and who I do business with. It helps isolate the projects and products that I build and work on.

It also minimizes the amount of noise that I experience in life. Even on a personal level, it helps me sleep better at night, knowing that I am not responsible for everything, but only a few tasks – both professionally and personally.

And as a result, I feel more fulfilled when I do them, which creates an outpouring of joy.

Learning that I don't need to be good at everything, as trite as it may sound, has been fundamental, and I'm so glad that I have been able to learn it as early as I did. I wish I had learned it earlier, but I'm not sure I would have taken it anyway."

I could not have said it better myself.

Be The Best At One Thing

Just like playing *Street Fighter*, you could spend a lot of time trying to learn every character's move set, or you can focus the same amount of time on one character and truly begin to understand how they play their best, to learn what moves and specials work well in which situations, and understand every possible match-up with just that one character.

This to me is a much greater payoff. Think back to something you do really well, something others compliment you on, but when you do it, it feels easy to you. Maybe others compliment you and ask how you make it look so easy. For you, it is just something you enjoy. This is the sort of activity you want to spend more of your time doing. This shows off your strengths, the areas where you are best. If you can find a way to do more of this activity in your day-to-day work, you will be happier and create better results for everyone else around you. The powerful question posed by Marcus Buckingham in *Go, Put Your Strengths to Work* summarizes this nicely: "How will I ensure that I put my strengths into play just a little more this week than I did last week?"

Now what about those weaknesses? What are the things you are not so good at doing? What are the things that are very difficult for you even though they may seem easier to other people? Remember, it is absolutely normal and okay to have weaknesses. The best thing you can do about these weaknesses is to overcome them by ignoring and focusing on what you are the very best at instead. If this is not possible, then find others who can help you, through being strong in areas you are weak.

LEARNING

"Death is inevitable. Our fear of it makes us play safe, blocks out emotion. It is a losing game. Without passion you are already dead."

Max Payne, Max Payne 2

Video games are an amazing learning tool, not fully maximized for all types of learning. Consider the amount of knowledge that a player picking up a new game has to face. Game rules, mechanics, names of characters, locations, enemies, goals, items, codes, button press combinations, and the list goes on. To enjoy a new video game, the player must undergo significant learning, often self-directed, and repeated with most new game purchases. Even when the core elements of the game do not need to be learned, as is the case with many sequels, time is spent on learning what has changed or is different from the previous incarnation of the game series.

In this way, video games are teaching principles, and much more than most realize. In relation to knowledge acquisition, here are some lessons that we can learn from video games.

The Downfall Of Every Video Game Villain

Learning is essential to growing. There is a subtle idea that has the potential to shape the entire direction that your life takes. A large number of video game villains have found their defeat at the hands of a hero who embodied this very trait. I would go as far as to say that the lack of this trait is the downfall of every video game villain. You can apply this same trait in your life and find that you will experience a transformation of your own. Consistent practice of this trait can create a person that is more likable to be around, approachable by others, and respected by those who know the individual.

Are you ready for this idea?

It is humility.

The best leaders have it. The best employees have it. The best organizations have it. The best heroes have it. While the common trait of a hero may be difficult to identify, almost every single villain demonstrates a high degree of arrogance.

It is worth pointing out that arrogance and confidence are not the same thing, but there is a fine line between the two. Arrogance is centered in pride, and typically reckless. Confidence is being self-assured in a realistic way and can co-exist with humility.

Humility is not the opposite of confidence, but rather, it is as author Ken Blanchard says: "Humility does not mean you think less of yourself. It means you think of yourself less." Embracing humility will enable you to learn and grow far beyond the individual who is prideful and arrogant. Only by letting go of pride can we learn lessons about *how* we learn from sources like the game *Tetris*.

Teaching With Tetris

Tetris is a timeless classic. Millions have indulged an obsession with dropping blocks to form an unbroken line. Even before *Angry Birds* and *Candy Crush*, non-gamers and gamers alike knew *Tetris*. Over 125 Million copies of the game have been sold. *Tetris* is pretty amazing. Its applications are near endless. For example, did you know that *Tetris* can:

<u>Help you stick to your diet?</u> Yes, *Tetris'* visual stimulation combined with its mental demands make for an ideal "pattern interrupt" when food or cigarette cravings hit.

<u>Help overcome Post Traumatic Stress Disorder?</u> A game of *Tetris* played within 6 hours of a traumatic event helps to weaken the vividness of the event, decreasing the long term impact.

<u>Help strengthen, and even grow grey matter in your brain?</u> Actually making you smarter and improving memory? MRI scans validated

177

that individuals playing *Tetris* for 30 minutes a day had increased thickness of grey matter, and improved efficiency of problem solving compared to those who do not play *Tetris*.

Beyond all that, *Tetris* even includes potential for an amazing technique that you can start using today to improve your focus and productivity. Before diving into this time saving technique, let me tell you a little bit about my background related to this classic Russian video game.

My History With Tetris

If you owned an original Nintendo Game Boy, then chances are you are very familiar with *Tetris*, since it was the original pack in game that came along with the system. The music for the game is instantly recognizable, and almost impossible to get out of your head. The Game Boy version also included a strangely memorable sound effect whenever your game ended. This sound always reminded me of a goat laughing at my misfortune.

I think one of the reasons I was even allowed to have an NES in the house was *Tetris*. It was one of the few games that both my parents loved. However, this became a challenge when you have to compete with your parents for screen time with the game. My mom and dad were both pretty good at *Tetris*, but they realized that enough is enough. When you start dreaming about blocks falling when you sleep, or see visions of them dropping every time you close your eyes, chances are it is time for little break.

How Your Work And Life Are Like Tetris

One thing that most people are not aware of, is that *Tetris* contains a fantastic technique for managing your focus and concentration at work. No, I am not suggesting you sit down and play *Tetris* at your desk. In most cases, having your boss walk past your desk while you are playing a video game is not likely going to end well. Sure there are some exceptions, but I really do not recommend it.

The secret to the time and focus management technique is contained within the play mechanics of the game itself. Consider the challenge you are faced with in a game of *Tetris*: you are literally responsible for making hundreds or thousands of decisions for how to place and position a wide range of different types of blocks, as they are falling with increasing speed. Imagine if you tried playing a split screen 2 player version of the game all by yourself, having to simultaneously turn, and align two blocks at the same time.

That alone would be very difficult but imagine if you were trying to handle a four player game of *Tetris* with four separate screens, simultaneously working four controllers to position four blocks – that would be just plain crazy!

But when it comes to taking on projects at work and multitasking in our own lives – this is exactly what we try to do!

Multitaskers Are Liars. All Of Them

Here is the part in the book where I offend self-proclaimed multitaskers. Multitasking is not possible the way that many claim (or wish) that it is. If you say you can multitask, you are lying. Studies have revealed multitaskers essentially take longer to do the same amount of things, with a lower degree of overall quality, than those who focus on one task at a time.

I have entered into some crazy debates with sincere people (or is that sincere debates with crazy people?) who whole heartedly believe they can multitask in the fullest sense of the word. It is impossible to dedicate 100% of your attention to more than one thing at a time. The mind does its best work when it is focused on one single task. If we tried multitasking in video games the way we try to multitask in real life, the foolishness would be quickly apparent. Back to playing four simultaneous games of *Tetris*, with four controllers, on four screens. Ugh.

Overcoming the mental noise that attempting to be a multitasker creates is at the heart of personal productivity master David Allen's excellent work *Getting Things Done: The Art of Stress-Free Productivity*. In this book, David Allen talks about how each of us have a brain that functions like a computer in a way – we have limited "Psychic RAM" that is, the mind can only hold so many things in its attention span at one time.

For this reason, we need to reconsider how we are using our mind. Our mind is more like the processor in a gaming console or computer, but its effectiveness is greatly hampered when we try to use it like a memory card or hard drive. During an interview that I co-hosted with Jared Easley, David Allen explained to us that, "our minds are for having ideas, not holding them."

Consider how overwhelmed you may feel sometimes. Think about every video game you want to play, every book you want to read and every movie you want to watch. Now think about everything you need to buy from the grocery store. Do you have any incomplete projects around the house? What about school work? All these thoughts take up mental energy. No wonder many of us feel overwhelmed and unsure of where to even start.

Worse yet, when we get a moment of free time, it is all too easy to waste it on something silly that we had no intention of even doing, like watching the TV, surfing the internet, or playing some crack-like addictive smart phone game. And then we wonder why we are not successful or why we encounter so many setbacks with the areas of life that matter most.

The Secret To Boosting Focus And Productivity

So here is the secret you and I can take away from *Tetris* and be much more successful, productive, and focused on whatever challenge or project we take on. *Tetris* only gives you one block pattern to deal with at a time. The game only allows you to do one of three things with the block in hand: You can rotate the block clockwise or counterclockwise, you can shift the block to the right of the left of the screen, or you can cause the block to drop faster. Once the block is positioned at the bottom of the screen, it is locked in place.

The display for the game is rather limited and distraction-free as well. There is a preview window up in the corner of your screen that shows you only the very next block that you will be able to control, and this informs the player as to what is coming next, but nothing more. Even throughout the dozens of updates to the game of *Tetris*, very little additional information is required, and that is a very good thing.

Within the game of *Tetris*, you need to make thousands of choices, but the game only allows you to focus your effort on one block at a time. The world's leading expert on personal productivity, David Allen, calls this idea "Appropriate Engagement." This means that the engagement, or focus, you place on the block you are controlling is significantly higher than the focus you place on the preview window. It would be an entirely inappropriate use of the player's focus to concentrate on arbitrary information, or worse yet, be overwhelmed by the sheer volume of choices that eventually need to take place.

Clearing Your Inbox Like A Stack of Blocks

A practical application of appropriate attention is the dreadful email inbox. If you are like many people I know, you will read an email that requires you to make a decision or take action, but instead, you close that email and move on to reading the next email before you make any decisions.

When we start opening up multiple emails, reading the contents, but not acting on it, we end up delaying the inevitable and we feel overwhelmed. At some point, we become so overwhelmed with so many different things to do, we don't even know what to do first. Once you have a few hundred or thousand emails backed up, your mind and motivation take a hard hit.

A more effective approach is to treat the email like a block in *Tetris*. Focus on just the message in front of you, then limit your available actions. Review the email and quickly make a choice about what do to with it. Responses to emails can be narrowed down to four categories. In this case, the more limited the actions you can take, the faster you will be able to deal with the email and move on, giving appropriate attention to each of the messages. The four response are: reply, delete, delegate, or save as a reference. The guiding principle for applying this approach is: if you can complete the task within two minutes, then do so before even opening the next email.

Here is a closer look at each of the possible actions that can be taken with an email.

Reply

Replying to emails is not always required, but if you notice that your response is needed, then compose a short reply and note any actions you need to take. Email is great for passing along information, but it is not always the correct medium for every communication. Carefully consider if an email reply will solve the matter at hand quickly, or if there might be a more appropriate channel for communicating your response.

Delete

This one is pretty easy. There are thousands of emails we receive all the time that require no action on our part whatsoever. Many emails, once read, can simply be deleted. Just as many emails can be deleted without even being read, and often you will find clues in the subject line that the message is just another piece of spam.

Delegate

Many emails require additional action to be taken, but it does not always have to be completed by you. Sometimes your action is relying the message to the correct person. Other times, emails include an action that you can outsource or delegate.

Save as a Reference

If you worry that the message contains information you might need to reference in the future, create a subfolder in the email inbox named "reference" for storing these types of emails. If there is a due date attached to it, set a reminder on your calendar to reference this message on the correct day.

Just like in *Tetris*, we perform our very best when we are focused on one task at a time, choosing not to worry about the next task until we have completely finished the task at hand. The email inbox is an easy example to use for understanding appropriate attention, but anywhere we divide our attention can stand to gain from a renewed focus and concentration.

185

COMMUNICATION & LISTENING

Say you what !!

Zero Wing

Translating video games from one language to another can present opportunity for all sorts of miscommunications. While not always concerned with essential information, mistranslation can lead to some humorous results – here are a few of the more memorable classic gaming mistranslations:

Metal Gear - I feel asleep.

Final Fantasy VII - This guy are sick.

Pro Wrestling - A Winner is You!

Dodonpachi - Violator and subject to severe penalties and will be prosecutedt to the full extent of the jam.

Ghosts n' Goblins - CONGRATURATION! This story is happy end.

Samurai Shodown 2 - Long, long ago, there were a man who try to make his skill ultimate. Because of his bloody life, it's no accident that he was involved in the troubles.

When you win a battle -VICTOLY !!!

Or the classic *Zero Wing* intro scene:

In AD 2101, War was beginning.

Captain: What happen?

Mechanic: Somebody set up us the bomb.

Operator: We get signal.

Captain: What !

Operator: Main screen turn on.

Captain: It's you !!

CATS: How are you gentlemen !!

CATS: All your base are belong to us.

CATS: You are on the way to destruction.

Captain: What you say !!

CATS: You have no chance to survive make your time.

CATS: Ha ha ha ha …

Operator: Captain !!

Captain: Take off every 'ZIG'!!

Captain: You know what you doing.

Captain: Move 'ZIG'.

Captain: (…)For great justice.

Ok, the last one had me laughing so hard that tears were flowing. But sometimes, mistranslation is not so funny.

Stepping Out Of The Game

During my junior year in college I had the distinct pleasure of visiting the country of Japan. This was a dream trip of mine. Truly a life-changing experience for me. I had the chance to spend over two weeks in Tokyo, living in the home of a friend. It gave me the amazing opportunity to see firsthand, what life in a Japanese home was really like, not just a tourist perspective, but that of a native. To anyone who has visited another country, the most authentic way to do so, is to stay in a local home (not a hotel).

One evening, we all gathered around the dinner table and enjoyed a delicious hot pot dinner. I remember making a comment to my Japanese friend that the meat was very different than the style I was accustomed to in the U.S. I intended this comment simply as an observation. Unfortunately, by the time it was translated back to my friend's mother, it somehow came across as a complaint.

Immediately, my friend's mother began profusely apologizing for dinner! I was horrified, and I handled the situation rather poorly. I became frustrated with my friend, and I blamed her for unfairly translating my comment, and rephrasing it in a way that, I thought, made me look bad.

I did the only sensible thing to do in a situation like this – leave the house and go for a walk. In the dark. In a country almost 7,500 miles from home, where I could not speak the language, and I only knew one other person.

Absolutely brilliant.

When my pride finally gave up, I returned back to my friend's house, only to realize, that while my words may have been mistranslated, my actions spoke far louder than my words. If there was any doubt about my maturity, this served to end the debate. While we might not face the same translation or word issues on a daily basis, it is often possible for what we say to be misunderstood by others.

How To Set Us Up The Bomb

Understanding the parts of a message is a good place to start. The ubiquitous percentile ranking of what messages are composed of, ranks words at 7%, tone of voice at 38%, and the remainder of our message is sent through body language and nonverbal cues.

Does this surprise you at all? The irony is we often spend so much time worrying about what words we will say, when that segment is actually the smallest part of communication!

Obviously, there are times when the words are very important, but this it is often dictated by the channel we choose to communicate through. What this means, is that we need to check that all three parts are working together when we are delivering a message. It also means that we need to give special consideration for what channel we choose to use for communication with others.

All Your Emails Are Belong To Us

If you have a really sensitive issue to discuss, or a topic that will generate discussion, then email is a poor choice. Email is best kept short, and based on facts that need to be communicated. Even the slightest hint of sarcastic wording or rudeness is dramatically magnified when you cannot use your tone of voice or body language to explain yourself.

Email works great for listing out responsibilities to many recipients, or any fact driven work with lists or bullet points.

Say You What !! The Telephone

The telephone is an appropriate channel when discussing issues that need immediate attention, and may require many questions or clarification required. Your body language can affect your tone of voice, so keep this in mind while on the call. If a lot of details are required, a follow up email is helpful.

In Person: How Are You Gentlemen !!

Whenever the time is available, in person meetings will provide the most complete method for communication. While not always practical or efficient, no other method provides as much opportunity to communicate across all three components of communication. It makes good sense to practice face-to-face communication skills whenever possible. Phone and email skills can improve from learning what works in person as well.

You Have No Chance To Communicate Make Your Time

Even the best communicators can be misunderstood, and the reasons for this are many. If you want others to understand your message, you need to start by focusing on what you can control, but also understand others bring their own thoughts, biases, and opinions with them. Communication is amazingly complicated, so much so that it is rather amazing how well we actually can understand each other. I also know, in spite of difficulties, working at communicating more effectively has always paid off for me. The classic quote from Stephen Covey is appropriate in workplace communication: "Seek first to understand, then to be understood."

Recovering From Miscommunication

Customer Service jobs can be very challenging, but that is usually due to just a few customers. I have spent several years working in the hospitality industry. I have worked as a waiter and expeditor in a fine dining restaurant, and worked at the front desk of a luxury boutique hotel. I have even worked in a call center, both on the phone and as a Quality Assurance Supervisor. In fact, almost every one of us is in the Customer Service business, in one way or another. Customer service can include how we respond to clients, customers, co-workers, or even our (Big) Boss.

We have all had those moments. You know, the moment when you realize that a customer you are dealing with is more than just a little unhappy. It can be difficult to connect with a person who is disappointed or who is feeling that their expectations were not met.

Sometimes it can be an easy fix, and other times it can feel like war.

Metal Gear Solid Close Quarters Customer Service

In the game series *Metal Gear Solid*, Snake (Solid/Naked) uses a form of combat technique called "Close Quarters Combat" or CQC. This particular approach allows practitioners to rapidly change between hand-to-hand combat and armed combat, typically a pistol and knife. Core to the style of CQC is disarming the opponent through grabs, holds and throws, often rending the combatant unconscious. In this way, CQC is very much about controlling the situation through redirection and leverage. This also gives the CQC practitioner an advantage when dealing with larger and stronger opponents, since size and strength are overcome by speed and body mechanics.

In other words, "hard" fighting styles are focused on head-on attacks, relying on a direct approach, while "soft" fighting styles emphasize redirection and can use the opponent's strength and momentum against them. CQC includes many of these "soft" elements. When it comes to dealing with difficult customers (or anyone, for that matter), it can be tempting to take a "hard" stance.

"I'm sorry sir, that's the policy."

"Because I said so."

But how well does that approach really work?

I know it might be easier to shoot a difficult person with a tranquilizer dart, but that really would not count toward making you a Customer Service expert (and I suspect this would be illegal in every place that I have been).

How You Can Use CQC For Customer Service

I want to share with you a proven technique that I have used when dealing with upset or disappointed individuals (in fact creator of the technique is a former English Professor, Police Officer, and Black Belt master of Karate!). In his must read book *Verbal Judo*, George Thompson provides an excellent framework for dealing with difficult interactions, and will allow you to channel your inner Solid Snake with some verbal CQC of your own. *Metal Gear Solid* Customer Service Training is inspired by *Verbal Judo*.

When confronting an upset or difficult person, remember the following acronym: "L.E.A.P.S."

Let's walk through each of the steps:

Listen

This is all about being present. Turn off the Codec or put away your phone and concentrate on the other person 100%. Not only is it important to listen, you have to LOOK like you are listening. Otherwise, you might make things worse and get blindsided by a biting comment or right hook.

Empathize

Empathy is about understanding where a person is coming from – it does not mean they are right, or even that you agree with them. The *Metal Gear Solid* series is particularly good at telling personal stories about the in game characters.

In *Metal Gear Solid 4,* members of the Beauty and the Beast Corps all have rather traumatic stories, including loss of their family to members of a cult, becoming a prisoner of war as a child, and even more terrible examples of how war can impact children. While you may be fighting for your life in the game, I could not help but feel a measure of empathy for some of my opponents.

When we demonstrate empathy for others, we show that we are understanding and that they can trust us to do what is in their best interest. This builds confidence and will help calm others down much more effectively than shouting "calm down!"

Ask

Make sure you ask questions to understand the problem, before jumping to conclusions. If the other person feels rushed, they will feel like you don't care. That will just make things worse, and slow down the process.

"I'd like to think we could solve this problem," is an example of a great message to share at this point.

While placing a soldier in a CQC hold, Snake is able to interrogate his captive or gain items from them. While I absolutely advise against placing a customer in a choke hold, I do recommend discovering what their expectations are and how things can be made right. It is always dangerous to jump to conclusions or try to solve a problem before the other person has even explained the nature of the problem. Even if you are right, you run the risk of upsetting them and delaying the whole process.

Sometimes we all just need to feel that someone else is listening.

Paraphrase

Members of Snake's support team often communicate over the in-game radio system, the Codec. Snake frequently repeats back important points, and often paraphrases in his own words what he understood.

This is a key action we should take to let others know that we have been listening, and that we are responding to their requests. Repeat the customer's words back to them to show you understand what they are asking or what they are upset about. This will also help if you have misunderstood something, as they will help get you back on track. Also, it gives the other person a chance to understand that you really are listening when you get it right.

Summarize

In a concise way, repeat the facts, express your concern for getting things back on track, and finally let the individual know what you are going to do to make things right. In the same way that Snake repeats back key points over the Codec, he often summarizes the next actions he plans on taking.

I know this all sounds so simple when it is written out like this, and the reality is that emotions run high and communication is very complex. As strange as it sounds, customers feel a high level of vulnerability, and this often comes out in anger, frustration, and fear.

Our goal is to ease that vulnerability through actions, and words.

And maybe a little Customer Service CQC.

An Acquired Skill

Can video games teach individuals to become better listeners? Improving one's skill at listening is something that can transfer over into any area of life. Rather than focus specifically on concepts like Active Listening, I would like to offer another way of listening for consideration. Specifically, listening to the music within video games.

Now at first, those not familiar with video games might find this to be a strange thought. In fact, if you are thinking about early games like *Asteroids* and *Combat*, there is very little music to speak about. Even the arcade and home games of the 80's and early 90's did not offer much in the way of a quality musical experience that general public might enjoy (I will make the point, *Mega Man 2* still has one of my favorite soundtracks on the original NES).

Enter The Epic Video Game Soundtrack

Much has changed since the "blips" and "bloops" of the early days, with high quality soundtracks to match the advancing visuals and story-telling found in many modern games. Would you believe the *Halo 4* soundtrack debuted on the U.S. Billboard at number 50? It is hard to imagine the Mario or Sonic soundtracks of the early 90's doing the same.

The first video game soundtrack that really stood out to me as being something completely amazing, was the Original Sound Track (OST) for *Castlevania: Symphony of the Night (SOTN)*. In fact, this was the first video game OST I purchased on CD. The OST for *SOTN* was the work of Japanese composer Michiru Yamane, also known for her work on the *Suikoden* series, as well as two of my favorite Konami games on the Sega Genesis: *Castlevania: Bloodlines*, and *Contra: Hard Corps*.

SOTN includes an incredible soundtrack of variety of different styles mixing rock, symphonic, acoustic, orchestral, and many other styles. The CDROM format on the Sony Playstation and the Sega Saturn allowed for more complex music in video games, now using traditional instrumentation rather than programmed sounds alone. One of my favorite pieces from the *SOTN* OST is "Wood Carving Partita," a harpsichord work that sounds like it could have been composed 300 years ago.

I enjoyed the music from *SOTN*, and this piece in particular, so much that many nights while I was attending college, I would leave the game playing with the TV turned off, using my stereo to continue to listening to this song as it looped throughout the night. I guess that means I listened to this track subliminally for a couple hundred hours (that is actually kind of weird). Then again, my son has been listening to video game soundtracks since birth, and his favorite lullaby is "Kids Run Through the City Corner" from *Final Fantasy VI.*

Unlocking The Joys Of Music

I want to offer you a masterful and life changing approach that you can use to unlock the joy of music, even beyond video game OSTs. The following is a life changing application of music appreciation by a gentlemen whom I admire greatly and has opened my ears further to the appreciation of excellent music of all kinds.

George Marriner Maull is a passionate advocate of classical music listener education and Artistic Director of The Discovery Orchestra. He is known nationwide for his televised Discovery Concerts and internationally for his weekly Discovery Orchestra Chats on YouTube. When I asked him "what is a life changing idea or habit for you?" he answered with the following:

> "Learning to listen attentively is a behavior I developed as a child. My earliest memory of being very emotionally moved as the result of music listening occurred pre-kindergarten. The occasion was the first time I encountered the sound of a symphony orchestra, albeit on an ancient sound reproduction device quite inferior by today's standards, a monophonic record player!

How it was that I was primed for this moment I cannot say for certain. Having a highly trained classical pianist for a mother undoubtedly played a significant role. As I continued to intentionally listen to all the music I encountered from that day forward, I came to be fascinated by the process of listening. I also began to notice that some people listened…and some people did not, and this intrigued me. Why did some people give music their complete, undivided attention while others read, talked or did other things while musical sounds were present?

Some answers would eventually come through my association with Saul Feinberg who taught music listening at my local high school. I'm going to repeat that – who taught music listening at my local high school. Dr. Feinberg was an unusual music teacher. There were other music teachers who taught choral or instrumental music, that is to say, they taught the performance of music. Saul taught music listening. And he did it very well.

Over the thirty years he taught at Abraham Lincoln High School in Philadelphia he influenced the lives of thousands and thousands of students – including me. I learned everything I know about teaching music listening from Saul. He called his course Perceptive Music Listening. And what did he mean by that? He frequently said that the more musical detail we perceive, the more pleasure we can receive from the experience of listening. And of course, right from the get-go, he made certain that his students perceived first-hand the difference between merely physically hearing music and actually giving music your undivided attention – or listening.

Learning to listen and having this behavior reinforced when Saul Feinberg said: "The more we perceive, the more we receive…" set the course for the rest of my life. Listening to music daily – and not just to classical music – has and continues to be perhaps the greatest source of pleasure and meaning in my life."

Putting This Idea To Work

Today set aside 10 minutes, giving your undivided attention to some music – no texting, no tweeting, no eating, no taking of cell phone calls or reading. Just listen. See what happens.

Each day this week, make the choice to be open-minded. Expand the kinds of music you are willing to try to listen to. Experiment with listening to some wordless, abstract music. Rather than notice what you do not like about a particular style, identify what you do like about it. Take 5 or 10 minutes to learn about some new aspect of music that you can notice from Discovery Orchestra Chats on YouTube or some other source.

Intentionally listen to (not just hear) some music every day. As you begin to notice more and more detail in music, become attuned to how the quality of your life is changing – hopefully for the better. Are you feeling more fulfilled? Are you feeling that your innermost self is somehow more fully expressed?

Most of us will not be musical performers…but we all can become perceptive music listeners, the result of a conscious decision on our part that will change our lives forever.

TEAMWORK & COLLABORATION

"So, Mr.Meteor, how does it feel to be famous instead of infamous?"

"Well, Wink, it feels great. But, I couldn't have done it alone…"

The Meteor, Maniac Mansion

Sixty-four percent of gamers indicate their family members play video games along with them, and online services have become all but mandatory in the latest generation of gaming consoles. This means that collaboration and teamwork are increasingly core skills required for successful gaming.

Teamwork and collaboration are both essential skills in today's global workplace. As organizations stretch across time zones and various physical locations, the ability to communicate, share ideas, and collaborate on work has dramatically increased. Technology has played a significant role in these developments, and I believe online multiplayer video games provide a glimpse into what collaboration could become.

This chapter will simply scratch the surface of the potential for applying teamwork lessons from video games, as I frame the proposed solutions as an answer to the question "Who is your player 2?"

The State Of Video Game Multiplayer Games

Some of my very best memories of gaming, and current experiences, for that matter, involve other players. There was something really special about the multiplayer games of the 80's and 90's. To start with, all the players had to be in the same room, usually using the same TV screen to play. I have always found it difficult to understand the argument that video games promote antisocial behavior. This is the case with any hobby. Fishing, stamp collecting, or binge watching episodes of TV shows like the *Walking Dead* are all possible hobbies that are just as likely, if not more, to promote anti-social behavior.

As previously mentioned, some of my best social memories involved video games. Many friends and I would play together in the arcade or at each other's houses, and beyond the actual playtime, we would talk about the games. We would discuss strategies, create new levels and power ups on paper, and discuss how we would change the game. We would interject the games' heroes and villains in to all kinds of different scenarios. Definitely not the type of antisocial behaviors video games are often criticized over.

I know a lot has changed. To start with, players are no longer required to be in the same room, or even the same country to play against each other. While this opens up the potential to meet new friends, a Bluetooth headset and online gaming just does not capture the fun of playing a game in the same room as your friends. Being in the same room is an awesome way to bond and have a great time. The energy and the shared experience often carry over into anything else you do while hanging out. In fact, some of the foundations of the book you are reading were developed during this time, when several of my friends and I were able to apply ideas from video games to help us successfully complete tasks at a job where three of us worked together.

Social gaming is a great way to have fun, get to know others, build real life skills, and stay out of trouble (for the most part). In fact, I have been able to make some great friends, thanks to our common interest in video games. Back when I was a teenager, it was also a great excuse to eat junk food and consume unhealthy quantities of caffeine. In retrospect, having stock in Pizza Hut and Mountain Dew would have really paid off.

Retro Gaming Multiplayer

Most gaming consoles of the 80's and early 90's only had 2 controller ports to start with, and many games were only designed to accommodate 2 players. There were several accessories that allowed you to add controllers for games that supported 4-5 players (*M.U.L.E.*, anyone?), but for the most part, multiplayer meant two players at a time.

So here is the important question: Who is your player 2?

Now I know we need to qualify what I mean by Player 2. There are three categories of Player 2 that come to my mind, grouped by the type and style of game you are playing.

- **Player 2 as Reciprocal/Companion – Fellow Traveler on a Shared Quest**

- **Player 2 as Rival/Challenger – Opponent to Overcome**

- **Player 2 as Role Model – Example to Follow; Coach**

Let's take a closer look at the first type of Player 2, filling the role of a fellow traveler on a shared quest.

Player 2 As Reciprocal/Companion – Fellow Traveler On A Shared Quest

The focus of this individual is **Teamwork**

In this case, Player 2 is the other guy or gal who is in the trenches with you. Together you are taking on the world, defeating the villain, and

207

saving humanity – or something to that effect. Great examples of games you would play together include: *X-Men: The Arcade Game, Knights of the Round, Contra, Metal Slug, Gunstar Heroes, Streets of Rage, Gauntlet, Smash TV* and the list goes on.

The two of you are fellow travelers down the same path, united by a common goal or objective. When one of you succeeds, you both succeed. When one of you fails, it brings you both down.

The Quest Before The Quest

When playing cooperative games together with a friend, often it would be a game that was new to both of us (usually a rental) and we would be facing these challenges together for the very first time. Brent Black (a.k.a. Brentalfloss) of *With Lyrics* fame and I both agree that Blockbuster Video store rentals were *the* source for some of the best memories and worst games. It is humorous how the scenario has universal application to many gamers who rented from the NES through Playstation era.

There you were in Blockbuster Video, looking for the latest hit game, only to find that it was already rented by someone else. So after searching around a bit, hoping that the game was just misplaced or that any moment it would be returned, you would finally settle on whatever was in stock. So how was this crucial decision typically made? Box art. Whichever game had the coolest looking pictures on the front of the box is what you took home with you. And so many times the game was absolutely terrible, but sometimes you got lucky and found a hidden gem.

Why Not Play Alone?

Many video games were so much more enjoyable with a friend joining you. The sense of wonder when fighting a huge boss, picking up a new power up, or discovering some new trick that would help both of you is a great feeling. It also encouraged experimentation with the rules of the game, trying to find new and creative ways to give the two of you an advantage against the relentless onslaught of whatever alien horde or ninja clan stood in your way.

Games that were painfully difficult, suddenly became much easier when you have the right Player 2. When playing a game alone, it was easy to get frustrated and give up, but with a companion I found that I kept my cool and could even joke about a game that would make me want to cry or hurl my controller against the wall while playing through single player mode. I noticed that something else would also happen. I would play better. Teamwork has a real multiplying effect, in video games and in life.

Ask To See The Cyborg Ninja's Resume Before Hiring

I am sure you have found out the hard way that not everyone makes a good Reciprocal Player 2. I know I have. When considering the best co-op players that I have shared epic journeys with, several traits came to mind:

Skill

An excellent Reciprocal Player 2 does not need to be better than you, but it sure helps if they are pretty good at the game. Especially in games where you share lives or player 2 can steal player 1's continues. You want someone who can keep from bashing your head in if your co-op game allows for friendly fire (I am looking at you, *Battletoads*).

Also consider matching up your strengths and playing styles to compliment each others' weaknesses. If you are playing *Final Fight* and one of you likes the slow, big, strong type (Mike Haggar, for example) a good compliment would be the quick, nimble, type (Guy). Together, the two of you present a much stronger team than either one of you on your own.

Generosity

Many 2 player simultaneous co-op games have limited lives and limited items to replenish health, so the excellent Reciprocal Player 2 will not scarf down that full pizza when he has complete health and you are about to die. The same holds true for power ups and items or weapons you find along the way. A greedy Reciprocal Player 2 can squander items and hurt the team's chance at being successful in the long run. They may see personal benefit in the moment, but this behavior catches up to you both.

Loyalty

When getting blindsided by evil ninjas, I want a Reciprocal Player 2 that will get them off my back, and who knows how to leverage teamwork to double team a boss. This Reciprocal Player 2 is always aware that the nature of the game is cooperation. You are one team, with one goal. It is not much of a co-op game if you spend your whole time watching the other guy play because he did not care if you survived.

And if you are this guy/gal, don't be surprised if your ignored (and now dead) teammate goes for a walk. Or "accidentally" hits the reset button/unplugs your controller (I would never do this. Ok, maybe once).

Who Is Your Reciprocal Player 2?

Everything that makes a good Reciprocal Player 2, also makes for a really good friend and co-worker. Take a look around you – who are your closest friends? Do they demonstrate loyalty, generosity, and skill?

What about you? How are you taking those around you into consideration, making sure that you are treating them in a manner that is fair, supportive, and reliable?

When you demonstrate these traits at work, with your spouse, and with your friends and family, the results are amazing.

The Second Type Of Player 2 – Rival Challenger

When examining the Reciprocal Player 2, we discussed the social aspect of gaming, and the importance of selecting the most suited type of Player 2 for cooperative gaming. We also discussed some practical ways we can cultivate the traits in ourselves that will take us down a path to being a more generous, loyal, and skillful person in how we deal with those around us. Next, we will look at the individual who is drawn closer to us through adversity. This is the Rival Challenger.

Retro Gaming Head To Head Multiplayer

I love a good head-to-head multiplayer game. One of my favorite genres, and the one that ate most of my arcade quarters, is fighting games. This was the main arcade draw of my teenage years; *Street Fighter II, Mortal Kombat, Virtua Fighter, Tekken, Killer Instinct, Samurai*

Shodown – I remember when each of these games were released for the very first time in the arcades.

Fighting games required a shift in mindset: you were no longer fighting off the computer for your hard earned quarters, you were battling against another human for the right to keep playing the game. And as the more powerful 16 bit home consoles (Sega Genesis, Super Nintendo, Neo Geo AES) became available, these battles moved to the living room TV. So when it comes to head-to-head video games, who is your player 2? Let's take a closer look at the second type of Player 2, filling the role of Rival/Challenger and as your greatest opponent to overcome.

Player 2 As Rival/Challenger – Opponent To Overcome

The focus of this individual is **Challenge**

In this case, Player 2 is the person standing between you and victory. One of the most common ways that I have enjoyed this type of interaction, is in head to head fighting games. While in games like *Final Fight* 2 and *Streets of Rage 3* you and your friend fought off computer controlled foes, the tables have now turned and you are battling each other.

Now this is not to say that you are turning your back on your friendship: quite the opposite, but it does represent a significantly different play style, and is best served by a different type of Player 2.

When it comes to fighting games like *Super Street Fighter II, Killer Instinct 2, or Mortal Kombat II*, the very nature of the two player game is that it is best enjoyed against another player of equal or slightly greater skill level. Now, of course it is no fun to get trounced in games like this, but when both of you are pretty closely matched in your skill level, it is an amazing rush. Something interesting happened as a byproduct of this level of competition. I learned how to play better. In the same way the support and encouragement of the Reciprocal/Companion type of Player 2 helps in cooperative games, equal or slightly greater skill levels help in the Rival/Challenger arena.

When going head to head, you learn tricks and tactics that let you improve your own game. And this is not limited to fighting games. *Super Mario Kart* or *GoldenEye 007* are both great examples of how healthy competition can be fun and make you a better player in the process.

Test Your Might

Just as there are specific traits that make for a superb Reciprocal Player 2, there are a different set of traits for an excellent Rival Player 2. Here are the attributes best suited for a competitive head to head player two:

Skill

In the Reciprocal Player 2, their skill kept you alive – in the Rival Player 2 their skill keeps you on your toes and pushes you to be better. Perhaps you have heard "As iron sharpens iron, so one person sharpens another." The perfect example of this is found in the balance of Ryu and Ken from *Street Fighter*.

Perfect rivals: neither one totally dominating the other, each with their own subtle strengths and weak points, able to balance and cancel out each other in a careful game of strategy. This tension is best if your Rival Player 2 is slightly better than you, but not so much better that you don't have any chance of winning. When there is a large skill gap, the better player will become bored and seek out greater competition. Such is the way of the warrior.

Good Sport

Another vital skill for your Rival Player 2 is temperance. If they are better than you and you manage to beat them, having a friend who will rage-quit or throw your controller against the wall is not cool. You may

215

even find them resorting to physical violence. I once knew a friend who said if they unplugged my controller or pushed me over as part of their strategy to win, it was totally fair. Needless to say, I did not play many head to head games with them!

Good Teacher

The very best in this category are willing to tell you how to do that secret move, show you the hidden pathway, or let you in on a better way of doing things. If your player two is a stuck up jerk who won't tell you how a move is done, it is time to move on to another player.

This is not as big of a deal now, since the internet has proliferated what were once considered tightly guarded secrets, but think about this: the writers of these FAQ's are exactly the type of sage that I am discussing. Without their generosity and teaching spirit, were would all be button mashing our way through many games. Thank you to the men and women who write game FAQs.

Who Is Your Rival Player 2?

The traits that makes a good Reciprocal Player 2, also makes for a really good business partner or competitive co-worker. Take a look around you – who pushes you to accomplish more? Do they demonstrate skill, a good nature, and are great teachers? What about you? How do you spur others on to action, encouraging them to do better and step up their game? Someone out there needs you to come alongside them and give a friendly kick in the pants.

Get moving! You're better than this!

The Third Type Of Player 2 – Role Model/Coach

While multiplayer gaming might initially conjure up images of cooperative shoot 'em ups, light gun games in the arcade, head to head fighting games, or first person shooter frag fests, there are also a large number of games that are one player in structure, but allow for turn based two player modes. Games like *1943*, *Galaga*, and *Super Mario Brothers*, are famous examples of two player games where both players wait while the other player takes their turn.

I would like to point out that sometimes this game play mechanism was used due to system or programming limitations. For example, the classic side scrolling beat 'em up game *Double Dragon* featured two player simultaneous action in the arcades and most ports, but was released with two player alternating gameplay on the Nintendo Entertainment System (The same holds true for *Final Fight* on the Super Nintendo).

Of course, you can always choose a "hot seat" approach, where you can play just about any game, taking turns by simply passing the controller to your friend. This is another great way to enjoy your favorite video game with a friend, and I have played through many of my favorites this way, even opting to play through some multiplayer games in single player mode with a friend – either to unlock game features, or because the game included a story mode that differed from the head to head gameplay.

So when it comes to turn based video games, who is your player 2?

Player 2 As Role Model/Coach – Example To Follow

The focus of this individual is **Mastery**

In this arrangement, you typically have a player who is more skilled or knowledgeable about the game (usually because I was playing it at their house and they owned the game). They have mastered some of the finer points, or are at least a few steps ahead of you. I found this was often the case, when we would play through a one player game together (like any of the *Mega Man* games), taking turns whenever the other person lost a life in the game.

The advantage here, is that the Role Model Player 2 has already made some of the mistakes before you even came over to play. They know which spikes can kill you, which pits have no bottom, which treasure chests are trapped, and where the hidden power ups are located. How do they know all this? Their time spent, experimenting, doing things the wrong way, even losing multiple lives - all work to your benefit.

When I play alternating video games with a friend who already has played the game for a while, something interesting happens. I learn how to play better.

Just like the support and encouragement of the Reciprocal/Companion and the equal or slightly greater skill levels of the Rival/Challenger boosted my skills, the wisdom and experience of the Role Model/Coach has helped me elevate my game. Nothing accelerated my techniques and skills faster than having an experienced player show me all the tricks and secrets they learned the hard way.

You have probably noticed that there is a bit of overlap when it comes to the different types of players – and no matter the type of game, you are better off when you have a player two that is skillful and willing to share what they know. The same is true in life. Surround yourself with others who are performing at least at the same level as you are. Do so in the professional sense, as well as the personal sense. The higher quality of individuals you surround yourself with, they great influence they will have on you.

And an interesting thing will happen.

You will be better for it.

Is It My Turn Yet?

Just like the previously identified types of Player 2, certain attributes stand out in my mind that make for a better Role Model two player experience. Here are some specific traits that make for an ideal Role Model Player 2.

Skill

The Role Model Player 2 has successfully mastered the game, or at least the gameplay mechanics. Ideally, the more they know, the better capacity they have to be an excellent Role Model. The experience and skill they have at a particular game is usually specific to that game. While they may be great at *Sonic the Hedgehog 2*, they may be terrible at *Rocket Knight Adventures*.

Leads by Example

If they can complete the level faster than you, then you can learn from them. It is a great way of building Self-efficacy – you gain confidence that you can complete a level/beat a boss/reach a difficult ledge since you observed them doing it. "If they can do it, so can I," is the thought process here.

Self-efficacy is a really important concept. It is task or game specific, but is a great way to learn. Have you ever been nervous when trying something new, only to discover that you now feel especially confident after doing the same thing several times? This is different than self-esteem, which is our feelings about things, often based on what happens to us. Self-efficacy means having the confidence that you can accomplish something, because you have done so in the past and you continue to improve as you do it.

Patience

The best Role Model Player 2 has a good deal of patience, since he has to wait for you to take your turn. Depending on his personality type, this can be especially tedious for him, since he must wait for you to finish before he can continue on with his rather impressive run.

The best Role Models enjoy seeing you improve your game, and will even offer tips and hints (when you want them). The "when you want them" part is important, because chances are you have played with the impatient version of this individual. You know the one – he is frustrated while watching you play, unable to believe how you just missed that checkpoint or wasted a shared resource in the game. Worse yet, he may even grab the controller away, saying, "let me do this."

This is the same behavior we see in a micromanaging boss, who cannot handle seeing his employees do things in a different way than expected. It doesn't matter how good he is (or thinks he is), no one enjoys an experience where they are being controlled.

Who Is Your Role Model Player 2?

The traits that make for a good Role Model/Coach Player 2, also makes for a really good boss or mentor in real life. In your professional life, do you know a skilled individual who leads by example, while demonstrating patience? They sound like a good candidate for a mentor! If you don't see this type of individual near to you, there are several things that you can do.

Look Outside Your Current Location

For the longest time, I thought a proper mentor needed to be my boss, or at least a higher-up in my own company. This often is the case when you start out and begin training in a new job, but as we advance in our career, it is a very good idea to connect with mentors outside of your own organization.

Crowdsource Your Mentor(s)

Another myth that I personally fell into, was the idea that my mentor had to be one specific person who was going to teach me everything that I needed to know about work, life, the universe, and everything. Let me know if you ever find this person. I don't think they exist. Or if they do exist, by the time I find them, it will be too late.

What I have learned instead, is to crowdsource my mentors. Find mentors who are the best in one area and learn about that area from them. If your boss at work is really good with time management and task management skills, focus on learning these specific approaches from her. You may need to find another individual to learn about people skills from – no one person will have all the answers.

Yeah, but… what if you don't know anyone who is good at anything?

First of all, this is probably not true, but for sake of argument, let's say that it is true. What do you do? There has never been a time in history when more knowledge, learning, expertise, and wisdom has been available. And so much is available for free. What you are reading right now is testament to this fact. In just the past two years, I have learned from over 100 experts in the fields of leadership, personal development, life skills, organizational development and psychology, and a great number of other topics. All for less than the price of one college course.

Become The Mentor

I am keenly aware of the lack of good, strong leaders. It is up to us to change that. The world needs leadership, it needs individuals who will step up and make a difference; leaders who will make the difficult choices, and do the right thing in the face of adversity; leaders who will be for others what they wish they had for themselves. This can be you.

It won't be easy, but it will be worth it.

And you don't have to wait for a "leadership" title to make this happen. It happens each and every day, in the small things, over time, and through the relationships we build.

Let's Play

As you can see, there is a lot to consider when choosing an optimal player two – a friend who is fun to play a side scrolling co-op game may not make the best rival in a game of *Samurai Shodown*. Likewise, your friend who can chain 5 hit combos into their Super AND Ultra Specials in *Super Street Fighter IV* is not the guy you want beating up on you when you are trying to complete *Streets of Rage 2* as a team.

For these same reasons, it is important to surround ourselves with connections, acquaintances, and friends who push us in the right direction, build us up, and push us to be the very best version of ourselves.

We also need to be looking at the person in the mirror, striving to be the best we can for others – to invest in them, support them, and encourage them to be their very best.

Massive Multiplayer Organizations

One-on-one relationships can be challenging, but when the team grows, so does the complexity. An especially poignant illustration for complexity is provided by Seth Godin in *Survival Is Not Enough*, where he identifies the inherent challenge of a committee. He begins by asking how many handshakes must take place in a three person meeting prior to everyone being introduced. Three is the obvious answer, but pay attention to the number when five people are in the meeting: the number swells to ten handshakes. By the time one hundred people are in a meeting space, it would take 4,950 handshakes for everyone to be introduced. Size quickly becomes a liability to speed.

While no fixed rule, teams of ten or less are desirable for flexibility and speed. With less individuals on a set team or committee, roles and responsibilities become crucial to success. While there are exceptions like the massive role playing game *Suikoden* where you can have 108 protagonists, most video games narrow roles down to a more manageable 4 or 5. One way that we can look at teams, and the tendency of individuals to choose or fulfill different roles on a team, can be seen in *Maniac Mansion*.

This Could Be Dangerous

A parody of science fiction and B movies, *Maniac Mansion* follows the story of teenager Dave, and two of his friends who are attempting a daring rescue of Dave's girlfriend Sandy. Sandy has been kidnapped by the stereotypical mad scientist, Dr. Fred who is under the control of a living meteor. The resulting adventure includes talking tentacles, a swimming pool filled with radioactive water, a mummified relative, and a hamster that explodes when microwaved (side note & bonus lesson: just because you can do something, does not that you should).

Working As A Team

Just like in *Maniac Mansion,* knowing your team members' strengths and weaknesses allows each individual to identify how they can best contribute. Dr. Meredith Belbin identified an existing "tendency to behave, contribute and interrelate with others in a particular way," when teams form.

It is also important to consider what happens when all team members are of the same style – imbalance occurs. While the team may be exceptionally strong in one area, they will also have an equally grand vulnerability.

In *Final Fantasy VI,* the team of adventurers encounter the Fanatic's Tower – a challenging location with great rewards. But there is a catch: the party can only use magic spells for offensive attacking. If the player has only been developing physical attack abilities up to this point, the tower will be a near impossibility. In the same way, if you rely exclusively on magic, you will find enemies who are invulnerable to spells, as well as the difficulty associated with depending on a resource that is finite.

In the workplace, teams that are too similar will spend more time competing for the work best suited to their style rather than co-operating on the work at hand.

Finding The Right Role

Dr. Belbin created three categories to group nine team roles. It is worth pointing out that all of the roles have both strengths and weaknesses. The goal is not to remove individual weakness, but to overcome individual weakness by combining group strengths. The three main categories are: Action Oriented, People Oriented, and Thought Oriented. Remember, these roles to not specifically related to personality type, but there is some cross over.

Action Oriented

Shaper (Dave)

Strengths – Get things moving, solving problems, sees obstacles as an exciting challenge

Weaknesses – May come across as pushy or argumentative

Implementer (Bernard)

Strengths – They make things happen. Systematic in approach and organized

Weaknesses – May resist change or deviation from the original plan

Completer-Finisher (Dave)

Strengths – Great follow up, attention to details and deadlines

Weaknesses – Perfectionism, difficulty is delegating

People Oriented

Coordinator (Dave)

Strengths – Guide the team towards objectives. Good listening skills and coordinates the team's contributions

Weaknesses – May be perceived as a manipulator and delegating more than they should

Team Worker (Jeff)

Strengths – Put the team and it is success first. They promote harmony and act as a diplomat

Weaknesses – Indecisive and may be unable to take a particular side, even when required

Resource Investigator (Wendy)

Strengths – Innovation, great for public relations, and enthusiastic

Weaknesses – Overly optimistic, able to become deflated easily

Thought Oriented

Plant (Chuck the Plant – sorry, can't help myself here)

Strengths – Unique and innovative ideas or ways of solving problems

Weaknesses – difficulty with criticism, tend to do best in solitude

Monitor-Evaluator (Razor, Syd)

Strengths – Analyzing and selecting ideas. Objective and can make strong decisions and strategic moves

Weaknesses – May come across as unemotional or cold

Specialist (Michael, Wendy)

Strengths – Expert knowledge or experience in a core area

Weaknesses – Limited knowledge or abilities outside of that topic

Bringing Sandy Home

A team can only explore its full potential when all roles are filled, providing a balance where the sum is even greater than the parts. The team can be even more effective and resilient when every member of the team knows their own role, as well as the role of others. This allows each group member to focus on what they do best, and seek out support from others where they are weak. If you are leading a team, it is important to notice the roles that each member is playing – awareness alone can help you solve and understand conflicts that might arise.

KNOWLEDGE SHARING

"Find something to believe in, and find it for yourself. When you do, pass it on to the future."

Solid Snake, Metal Gear Solid 2

Poor communication and lack of sharing knowledge are often cited as reasons for significant frustration within the workplace. Up to 86% of employees reported poor communication as a cause for failure, with 97% agreeing that lack of alignment in a team will have a significant negative impact on the outcome of a project. The workplace is filled with pitfalls for communication and alignment. As a broad generalization, video games have done an effective job of addressing many barriers to communication and alignment.

The way that most video games are designed conditions game players to expect, and even thrive on up to date information. As a whole, the near-instantaneous flow of information and feedback from video games is unrivaled by even the best organizations in the business world.

In modern games, the information is timely, focused, reoccurring, and self-revising. In game map systems have demonstrated a user friendly interface and accuracy the GPS industry only wishes it could have. Heads Up Displays (HUD's) in video games offer more than just large amounts of data, they offer specific and relevant data, often with real time progress indicators. The ability to communicate and share information on the fly with this same degree of accuracy and flexibility could change almost any industry.

In *The New How,* Nilofer Merchant describes how communication and alignment can boost buy-in from team members within an organization and increase the energy level in the process, "Everyone is better off when they know why decisions are made with as much accuracy as possible. It gives them an understanding of what matters and provides information on which to base the trade-offs constantly being made at every level." With all the details and important information flowing across any business or organization, how does one determine what is shared, what is valued, and who needs the information? The starting point is asking these clarifying question from the very beginning.

Creating Clarity

Overcoming misalignment is as simple as creating clarity through simplicity. Easier said than done, right? Before proceeding, it is worth noting that simplicity is different than simplistic. When something (or someone) is labeled as simplistic, it is typically done so in a derogatory manner. Calling someone simplistic to their face is tantamount to calling them stupid. Not the best way to be addressed.   Simple, on the other hand, is about being comprehendible. A quote that is often misattributed to Albert Einstein explains this concept succinctly: "If you can't explain it simply, you don't understand it well enough."

Consider how a video game like *Pong* demonstrates both simplicity and clarity:

Simplicity: You are a paddle, your opponent is a paddle, and the two of you are hitting a ball back and forth.

Clarity: If the ball goes past your opponent's paddle, you get a point. If it goes past your paddle, they get a point. The first to 11 points wins.

Ever wish that your job was that simple? Sure, it might get boring after a while, but there are some days that I long for this degree of simplicity. Consider the efficiency and focus of a game of *Tetris*. Life is not always that simple. As much as I criticize specific elements of *Final Fantasy XIII*, the game can teach us a lot about the importance of clarity and focus in life.

3 Questions to Clarify And Simplify Your Leadership And Life

Now a word about leadership – if you influence other people, you are a leader. And the best leaders provide clarity and simplicity. In *Final Fantasy XIII*, we see Claire Ferron a.k.a. Lightning as a leader for much of the game, but others step into the leadership role as well. Leadership expert Andy Stanley points out three questions that anyone can ask of their organization, department, or even themselves to provide greater clarity and accomplish more. The three questions Andy offers up are: "What are we doing? Why are we doing it? And where do I fit in?" Allow me to reference the world of *Final Fantasy XIII* to provide an illustration of these questions in practice.

What Are We Doing?

In the world of *Final Fantasy XIII,* the god-like race known as the *fal'Cie* assign tasks to chosen individuals. The individual who is assigned the task is marked with a brand on their body that changes over time, and becomes known as *l'Cie.* The *l'Cie* are given a very specific purpose or "Focus." While the specifics of the Focus are not always given in full initially, every *l'Cie* has the responsibility to carry out this task which is unique to them.

In the workplace does everyone on your team understand what you are doing? I had the chance to attend a Ritz Carlton training session in Washington, D.C. where I saw firsthand how the organization elegantly summarizes their mission statement in a way that everyone in the organization can repeat it and live it.

"We are ladies and gentlemen serving ladies and gentlemen."

Powerful, and I still remember it to this day. Anyone at any level can appreciate, understand, and do amazing things with clarity.

Think about some of the early role playing and adventure games from the 80's. I spent so much time just wandering around with no clue where to go or what I should be doing. *Castlevania 2: Simon's Quest* and *Faxanadu* were both pretty horrible about explaining what you needed to do next. There was no Game FAQs to check, everything was trial and error. Lots of error. Sometimes the workplace can feel the same exact way. The number one reason why employees don't do the most important thing at work, is that they think they think they already are doing it.

The problem with an absence of information is that the human mind is challenged to fill in the blanks. The mind will fill in the blanks, but it will be each with individual's interpretation. If you expect others to read your mind or fully appreciate your vision without significant communication efforts, you are setting yourself up for massive disappointment and failure.

Why Are We Doing It?

If only I stopped and asked this question of myself more often. Have you ever stopped to ask why your job exists? What about the department you work in? At some point your title and department were created to meet a specific need – if you can connect to that, the purpose will become much clearer.

In most video games, our "Why" is pretty clear. Have you seen the opening of *Double Dragon*. Thugs punch and kidnap a girl. Billy Lee & Jimmy Lee appear in a fight stance. Is there really any need to say more? If only your "Why" was more obvious in everything you do. *Final Fantasy XIII* gives **crystal** clarity (sorry, could not resist) to the Why, as each of the members of your party are branded and imprinted with a "Focus."

When we understand the Why, the What we do and How we do it become much more clear. Simon Sinek refers to this concept as "The Golden Circle." The team member who understands Why something is being done is freed up to innovate, motivated to act, and inspired to make a difference. In the absence of understanding the Why, individuals are left to identify their own Why. If they cannot find an inspiration to continue doing a specific task or role, they will seek out another role or organization to align themselves with. This tends to be most true with the individuals who you would least want to leave.

Where Do I Fit In?

On a more personal level, it is time to figure out YOUR role. What possible unique contribution can you make? Think about the combination of talents, gifts, and experiences you have – all together, no one else can do the things you can. As we see with the strengths-based mindset, don't try to be someone you are not – try to be even more of who you are.

Most video game characters have unique skills and roles, abilities which allow the hero to be the hero. It does not mean you are perfect but it does help you find the perfect role for you. Snow in *Final Fantasy XIII* plays the role of the Sentinel. His purpose is to draw attention to himself and absorb damage, thereby protecting the other members of the team who can focus on healing and attacking. He is well suited to this role, with a naturally higher amount of health and durability. If no one takes on the role of Sentinel, the entire party can be wiped out very quickly. Not every role is glamorous, but all are important.

Sometimes The Best Example Is A Negative Example

Clarity does not guarantee success, but it makes it much easier to stay focused, motivated, and on track. Snow gives us a great example of what not to do as a leader when he says: "Since when have heroes ever needed plans?" Failing to plan is planning to fail. A great way to lead is to make a plan to communicate to your team What you are doing, Why you are doing it, and How they fit in.

PERSISTENCE & GRIT

"These are my parting words to you; those who give up are doomed."

Anna, Phantasy Star II

Perhaps the most valuable transferable skills that are all too often overlooked from video games to reality are the ideas of persistence and grit. Both these traits are almost universally required to be successful in any game that is on the market. The same also holds true when it comes to achieving anything worthwhile in life.

Before I go much further, I realize the need to define the term "grit." My favorite definition of the term comes from Angela Lee Duckworth's TED talk on the topic: *"Grit is sticking with your future — day in, day out, not just for the week, not just for the month, but for years — and working really hard to make that future a reality."* Game designers, writers, artists, and those in creative careers know this struggle all too well.

This capacity to be able to withstand challenges in increasing levels is the exact sort of skill that needs to be developed to be successful in the long term, but often times requires the actual experience of increasing challenge. The greatest challenge faced with feats requiring this degree of persistence is they often come at great cost, especially if the individual is unsuccessful in overcoming this challenge.

It is not often that most of us would be willing to take a dramatic risk that could potentially end our careers, impact our livelihood, or even result in the loss of our life itself. Most of us just don't have the tolerance for that degree of extreme risk, at least not voluntarily.

The good news is extreme resilience this can be developed in almost any video game found on the shelf today. Video games are problem solving simulators where individuals are faced with increasingly scalable difficulty against insurmountable odds. As storylines, voice acting, and in game cinematics have rapidly improved, opportunities for emotional connection and impact have greatly increased. It is not uncommon to speak with gamers today who can tell you about being moved to tears by the plot or events of a video game.

The Success Trait That Video Games Already Teach Us

Video games often get a bad rap for being a waste of time, contributing to antisocial behavior, or even inspiring terrible violence. Often overlooked is their potential as an unrivaled source of learning and an untapped mechanism for teaching life principles. In fact, I believe that many individuals who enjoy video games are routinely practicing desirable traits that can lead to real world success, if they are correctly applied. The one trait that is the most notable as it relates to success in all areas of life is the idea of persistence.

Video games are an amazing source for teaching persistence. Think about a difficult video game that you have beaten. You had to face overwhelming odds, often times acting as an individual or part of a small team to save the world, or even the universe. You were only successful because you did not give up.

Adults who are in their late twenties up through their forties have experienced some of the most challenging digital tests of persistence known to man. High difficulty, limited resources, and rules that could erase hours' worth of effort are familiar aspects of video games for those of us who grew up with *Castlevania III: Dracula's Curse, Top Gun, Yo! Noid, Ghosts 'n Goblins*, and *the Silver Surfer.* An iron will, practice, and persistence were required to ever see the ending screen of many games from the 80's and 90's.

And this persistence places us in good company.

History Remembers Persistence

Consider for a moment the universal trait of world changing people like: Martin Luther King Jr., Gandhi, Mother Theresa, and Albert Einstein. All shared this virtue in common: persistence. While I appreciate that beating *Double Dragon III* is nothing that would warrant the honor of a national monument, I do wish to explore the opportunity of potential for real world success, based on a concept developed through playing video games.

Consider a more modern example from the musician, Klayton (Celldweller) who embodies the very idea of persistence in his life and career path. Facing incredibly difficult odds and an industry that has done him no favors, he essentially built his career during one of the most difficult times of change in the history of music: the digital revolution. Remember Napster anyone?

In spite of opposition from music labels, so called "fans," and naysayers at every turn, Klayton successfully created his own record label and positioned his own brand of music in countless Film, TV and video games (*Assassin's Creed 2*, *Dead Rising 2*, and *Need For Speed: Most Wanted*, to name a few). When asked about his advice to others in a 2013 interview by The Music Ninja, he said the following: "PERSIST! The only reason I am here today is because I was too dumb or stubborn to quit the many times that I was told to or circumstance probably suggested."

The element of persistence is vital in the many roles we all face. When I consider my success in the various roles and responsibilities of life, persistence was at the heart of every win. Here are a few examples from my own experience.

As A Husband

If it was not for my persistence, I never would have ended up with my wife. In fact, our very first date only happened when I took the initiative to put myself out there. Knowing I was way out of my league, I had to make it difficult for my future wife to say, "no." At the time, I had no idea where she lived, other than knowing the general area. I got in my car and started driving, and then called her on the phone. She told me that she was going out that night with some friends and family, but they were getting ready to leave soon. I asked if I could join them, since I was already in the area (never mind that I had driven 40 minutes to be "in the area"). Six months later we were married. She later told me she loves that I was persistent this way. Almost twelve years later now, a different kind of persistence is required to remind her how much she is loved, even with crazy schedules, work, and a toddler who seems to never sleep.

As A Father

I see this as an incredibly important lesson to pass on to my son. As he is learning to read, patience and persistence is absolutely necessary. I have to model for him how important it is not to give up when things are difficult, but to keep trying and sometimes take a new approach when one method is not working. It has been so rewarding to watch him do more and more for himself as he is developing a trait that I know will be key to his success in life.

As An Employee

In any season of your work life, persistence pays off. Looking for a job? Be persistent in your search, and pursuit of the job you want. Looking for a promotion? You have to be worth more before you can earn more, so persistently seek out opportunities to provide value and make a difference. Are you content with where you are in your career? Chances are you only got there through persistence, and you will not stay there long if you do not persist in the behaviors responsible for putting you there in the first place.

It took me three different tries of re-writing my own job description and building a case before I received a promotion in one job that I worked. Looking back, persisting in asking myself the question "what can I do differently to make this happen?" was vital to achieving the outcome I desired. It is true that when you want something badly enough, you will persist until you make it reality. The challenge is to examine what it is you really want, so when you meet resistance you are able to persist.

As An Entrepreneur

Here's a bold claim: no entrepreneur can be successful without persistence. Starting anything new is scary and risky. The temptation to give up or give in can be overwhelming. In the very beginning excitement levels run high, and early results of your effort are motivating. The most difficult time for an entrepreneur is during the period Michael Hyatt refers to as the "messy middle." Many video games can provide inspiration for how to overcome this area with proper pacing and creative milestones.

Video games are really good at celebrating the steps along the way, even in ways that are as simple as the positive encouragement like the words: "you win!" special animations, music, story cutscenes, or unlocking new items, weapons, tools, or equipment in pursuit of your goal. All these features give a sense of payoff for your hard work.

As an entrepreneur, you need to build these same concepts into your work. Be intentional with your goals and milestones, and remember to celebrate. Nothing motivates like a sense of winning early on in a project or new venture. As CEO of Apple, Steve Jobs once said, "I am convinced that about half of what separates the successful entrepreneurs from the non-successful ones is pure perseverance."

Consider an element that started out in role playing games but has spread to just about every genre of video game: leveling up. Defeating enemies or completing challenges provide "experience points" that move the player towards the next "level" for their in-game character. Many games scale the experience needed to level up based on your current levels or the amount of progress you have completed so far. Like the example given earlier, moving from level 1 to level 2 takes very little time when compared to moving from level 50 to level 51.

This is why celebrating the success and advancement from the early stages is so important. Quick wins inspire.   Failing to set milestones along the way can kill the motivation needed to persist.

How Video Games Help To Build Persistence

Another key factor in persistence that video games can teach us is the required element of hope. Part of what keeps us motivated in playing video games, is the hope or expectation that what we are trying to do actually can be accomplished. If a video game had no ending, or measurable success was impossible, most individuals would lose interest very quickly.

That is why points, items, trophies, achievements, and unlockable bonuses in video games are so important. They give us hope that our persistence will pay off. The outcomes and pay offs in life are not always as apparent. Sometimes, the rewards of persistence are found in the absence of certain consequences.

Next time you face a challenge, remember if you were playing a video game, the obstacle would never keep you from winning. Vince Lombardi said it well: "Winners never quit and quitters never win." Years later, Lightning from *Final Fantasy XII* said, "It is not a question of can or can't…in life there are some things you just do." Our roles in life are far more important than our roles in video games, but if we examine and apply the lessons that make us successful in video games, real world success will soon follow.

Joust Can Get You Promoted

Along with grit, a determining factor in success in life, school, and work (as well as a determining factor in getting a promotion) is a strong sense of urgency. So what is a sense of urgency? Focusing on what matters and immediately seeking out to resolve it. Sometimes failing to do so can lead to a missed opportunity. Other times, not having a sense of urgency means a Pterodactyl will come out of nowhere and knock your butt off of your ostrich.

Move It, Bird Knight

In the game of *Joust*, your goal is to take out the other bird knights by, sitting on their heads. You can try poking them with your lance, but sitting on them seems to do the trick (and is a lot safer, too). Meanwhile, the world is basically falling apart around you, with platforms disappearing and ground turning into open lava pits.

Once you have accomplished an avian takedown, you must pick up the egg that drops from the bird for points, but more importantly, if you ignore the egg, it will hatch a new knight (!?!?) who will mount a new bird – and try to kill you. I can only imagine how badly I would want revenge if someone knocked me off of a bird so hard that I had to hatch from an egg to come back.

Taking out Bird Knights, making omelets before eggs hatch, and avoiding a micromanaging boss Pterodactyl – everything in *Joust* is about developing a sense of urgency. This same quality applied to your job is a key to productivity, success, positive self-esteem, and is one of the traits employers often base promotions on.

Creating A Bias For Action

Like any game with a timer, a sense of urgency is more about competing against yourself – trying to get things done right, but as fast as you can. Leadership expert Brian Tracy points out the value in harnessing this "bias for action," as he calls it.

"You take action rather than talking continually about what you are going to do. You focus on specific steps you can take immediately. By employing this technique you concentrate on the things you can do right now to get the results you want and achieve the goals you desire."

This is immensely powerful. Focus on what you can do, here and now, then set out to do it immediately. It is far too easy to procrastinate and put things off because we are "waiting for the right time" or we are "not sure what to do," so instead we do nothing.

Making it Work for You

What is something you are dealing with (maybe something that is stressing you the most)? What is the very first action that you can take right now towards completing it?

Now go do it. Really, it is that simple. You are now one step closer to being done – and since you are in motion, each action you take next will become a bit easier.

Check Your Attitude And Altitude

Just one more note about a sense of urgency. In head to head fighting games against other skilled players, there is a lesson which becomes incredibly obvious: remember to check your emotions and motivation before taking action. If you jump into something out of impatience, anger, or frustration you will most likely make some bad choices. Bad choices are not the end of the world, but the goal here is positive movement, not experimenting. The underlying motivation for success has to be a desire to win, to overcome, and every action should support this movement.

Just like flying an ostrich, momentum is a powerful force – it can be very difficult to change direction mid-flight – so make sure your direction is correct, then make adjustments as needed. One of the major determining factors in winning the game of *Joust* is your altitude: when you collide with another Bird Knight, whoever is higher up, wins. This is exactly true with your attitude – keep it high, and success is yours.

CONCLUSION

"Every story must have an ending."

Auron, Final Fantasy X

The content covered in this book is only scratching the surface. For every industry, video game, and video game player there are countless application of the principles that lead to success. The key to identifying these opportunities and lessons require that we pay careful attention to the world around us. This is difficult, since it often seems like life is set on the full speed turbo setting. The danger here is that we turn off our brains and switch on autopilot. I worry that too many individuals are content to disable their ability to think and just follow a path that is laid in front of them. Risk can lead to failure, and the fear of failure can lead many down a path of just playing things safe.

Asleep At The Controller

I love multiplayer games. Being able to compete with your friends in a 4 player game of *Perfect Dark* or *Bomberman* on the Nintendo 64 is amazing fun. Online connectivity has opened the doors to the world, and we can now test our skills against challengers from across the country, or even form a team with real time communication across the globe. But the online gaming experience brings a new frustration with it. The absentee gamer. Are you guilty of this online gaming sin?

You know the guy – he sits in game lobbies, but never seems to hit "start." Their name and avatar show up in game, but no one is at the controls. If they are on the other team, or you are playing a free for all, they make an easy target. But if the game depends on them to move forward, everyone suffers. I used to run into the problem frequently while playing first person shooters on my PC. I also find myself wondering why players in *Street Fighter IV* set up a lobby only to leave it unattended.

What about in real life? Have you ever been speaking with another person, and it feels like they are "not there?" More than just mental "lag," they are physically there, but it is as if they have projected their brain into another body and went out for lunch. Maybe she is checking her phone while you are talking to her, or maybe you keep looking over his shoulder while he is talking to you. I know I do the same thing too.

Another person is talking to me, but I am still thinking about work, my plans for the weekend, what I am going to make for dinner, or a long list of games I own but have no time to play. Sometimes, it is pretty obvious when we are not present. Your body is there, but your mind is in some other place.

Pause. Focus. Unpause.

I am a parent and I have a busy schedule. I work full time, I am a husband, a father, a member of a professional organization. I take my son to karate lessons, I read books, I am involved with my church. I write, play video games, and spend time with friends…and much more. We all have very busy lives, but are we present where we are? When we interact with friends, family, customers, speak on the phone, or participate in a meeting, it is vital that we are present.

This means 100% of your attention is in the right place. Often times, when we let our minds wander, we engage in wasteful or even dangerous thinking. We stir up anxiety about things we cannot change or control. In a FPS, that's a good way to get fragged. Don't be guilty of this online gaming sin in real life.

Achievement Unlocked: Showing Up

Focus has some other great benefits as well. Even if I am feeling down, I have found that if I put all my focus and energy into what is right in front of me, if I try to do my very best, I see great results and I feel good too. In fact, this is one of the very best ways to get your mood back on track. Take some time today to slow down, enjoy the moment, and be present. Time is fleeting, enjoy each moment for what it is. If you put this idea into practice, every relationship you have will be better for it.

You Must Overcome Fear, To Be Awesome

Once we increase our focus, we are able to take on fear. *Galaga* can show us how. Like *Joust* and *Tetris*, the rules of the game are simple, but the implications are profound. One feature that made *Galaga* really interesting was the alien ship equipped with a tractor beam – it would fly down and shoot a wide, slow moving ray that could capture your spaceship and recruit it for the other side. At first this seems like a fate worse than death. Until you realize that you can get your ship back and double your firepower in the process!

I still remember the sense of wonder when I first saw this accomplished. I remember how awesome I felt when I would show off this move to someone else who had no idea what was going on. It was a risky move, but it was awesome and it let you do awesome things. Sure, it could go wrong. Your former ship was now used against you. You could lose your ship by shooting it accidentally, or having it crash into you.

Avoiding this scenario was safe. It was average, and it is boring. Life can follow this same path. We can default to playing it safe, not taking risks or chasing our dreams. Content to live out our existence, in a safe, boring manner, we allow fear to stop us from advancing to a state of awesomeness.

How Fear Holds Us Back

Fear is a nasty little thing, bestselling author of *Start: Punch Fear in the Face, Escape Average, Do Work that Matters*, Jon Acuff points out that fear tries to defeat us whenever we try to do something awesome by attacking us with three basic messages:

1. Who are you to do that?

2. You're too late

3. It has to be perfect

Jon asserts that fear and doubt are just like muscles: Every time you believe a lie about yourself, it gets easier to believe the next time. I have to admit, I experienced all of the three voices listed while writing this book. While I have managed to overcome the first two messages with increasing success, I still struggle very often with wanting to make sure something is absolutely perfect before I go forward with it. Perfectionism leads to procrastination, and that keeps us trapped in fear.

Video games can actually be a safe way to try things out, without the extreme risks that we find in life. But let's be clear – accomplishments in a video game are no substitute for real world results. This is an area that can be very dangerous and deceptive.

Overcoming Fear To Be Awesome

Jon has two simple, yet excellent, actions you and I can take every time that fear gets loud. By the way, when you are trying to do something of significance fear shows up big time – and its presence can sometimes be reassurance that what you are doing matters.

Write Out The Fear Statement

Next time you take a step forward and you hear something like "who are you to do that?" or "who is going to care about this anyways?" write out what is in your mind – get it down on paper. It is amazing how silly or obviously wrong these statements sound once they are out of our head.

Share What You Are Hearing

I love the way that Jon talks about this step. Fear hates a sense of community – fear can do the most damage to us when we are alone and isolated. In fact, one of the statements I have caught myself thinking sounds like this: "They will think you are silly for even being afraid to do that. Better keep it to yourself."

Now it is important that you share with people you can trust, or are mature enough to admit their own fears and doubts as well, but don't let that keep you from making the effort and reaching out – you will be surprised by how many other successful individuals feel the same way.

So take a risk, let the tractor beam pull up your spaceship, then in epic fashion, steal it back and be awesome.

Where Is This Going?

Video games may be called many things, but denying their potential for teaching is short sighted and foolish. It may not be practical on a large scale to inject life or business lessons into existing video games, as this requires very specific knowledge on both the part of the teacher and the learner. A more practical and pragmatic approach would be creating a video game that is fun and engaging, but designed to include core concepts in a fashion that is allegorical. This is a significant opportunity for stealth learning that could be just as compelling as any storytelling video game.

The Next Thing In Gaming

I am noticing a trend of independent video game developers working toward this particular approach with an increasing number projects that focus on "Empathy Gaming," where the goal is to develop a sense of empathy for others by creating a simulated experience for the player. Games like *That Dragon, Cancer* exhibit a maturing of how we think about what a video game is, and how we can understand and connect with the human experience, and even matters of faith, though this relatively young medium.

257

This is really only the tip of the iceberg. The potential behind this idea, I truly believe, is near unlimited with all the aforementioned strengths standing behind video games, the greatest question that is on my mind is how much longer before its advantages are truly leveraged to maximize to their full potential? The barriers I see involve the commercial nature of video games.

In the recent years video game budgets have swollen exponentially with AAA level games like *Assassin's Creed*, *Grand Theft Auto V*, and *Call of Duty: Advance Warfare* costing in the tens if not hundreds of millions of dollars to produce. Inevitably, these games fall into the trap of being iterations of the previous game with publishers looking to simply capture the same audience that previously purchased the last title of the series.

It seems this strategy is truly reaching its tipping point. The latest entries into the *Call of Duty* and *Assassin's Creed* franchises are prime examples of what happens when a game studio has run out of ideas, yet continues to produce an updated iteration of their last game on a regular basis. Even Nintendo's first party games have fallen into this rut as of late. The reasons for this are pretty obvious: it is more about creating the next blockbuster product with a quick turnaround time for developing while making money off of the similar or previously proven idea than it is about innovation and pushing the envelope.

The larger the game's budget, the more risk adverse the publishers tend to be with the game itself. With all that in mind, what happens when the small, independent developer creates a game as a labor of love? We end up with some pretty amazing things.

For us to truly change how video games are used and what their role is in learning, we need to have a fundamental shift in our understanding of both the purpose of the video game and its true potential. When we realize that a game can be more than just killing zombies, shooting enemies, or destroying objects, and embrace that a game is the very best place for epic narratives and storylines that don't have violence as a de facto mechanism for gameplay, we can begin to make progress. Sure, there will always be a place for this type of game, but what we too often miss is that video games can, and should be, so much more.

Games like *To The Moon* use a familiar traditional format for gameplay but lack combat altogether as part of its story. The aforementioned *Journey* and *Flower,* also by the same studio (Thatgamecompany) are both examples of games which can provide a compelling narrative or entertaining gameplay without falling into the stereotypical traps many video games still find themselves bound by. Creating a truly breakthrough concept and a video game though is very risky and until the market has proven that it has a taste for unique and innovative approaches, my fear is that we will continue to see more of the same before it gets better.

Mature Content And Maturity Are Different Things

In a recent interview, blogger and podcaster Ellory Wells asked me about my thoughts on mature content finding its way into video games. I think there is an important distinction to make when answering questions like this - mature content does not necessarily represent mature ideas. The violence, language, nudity and sex within video games has exceeded the maturity levels of the art form. When it comes to handling those issues, growth still needs to happen for video games to be taken seriously as a works of art. I realize this is a sweeping generality, but it is also an honest one in regard to how video games are perceived, especially by those who have no interest in playing them.

My Closing Thoughts

While I don't believe video games are the only solutions to the challenges that face us I believe they can offer insight into many possible solutions.

Is it possible that one day a publisher will create a game that can teach truly transferable skills to those who play? Absolutely. But this day may still be quite a ways off. In the meantime, it is important that those of us who find ourselves in leadership roles, managing others, or looking to leave the world a better place than how we found it, are able to take these concepts and apply them. It is important that we are able to think creatively and look for ways our hobbies can help us be successful against the greatest challenges that face our generation.

Video games are fantastic problem-solving simulators, and as gamers, we need to take the same mindsets that have helped us be so successful in our hobby and begin applying them to other environments. In the process, we may find out that reality can be just as fun as some of our games, and the rewards are much longer lasting. After all, it would be a real shame to let those 10,000+ hours we have spent playing not be fully leveraged when there is more that we can learn from them.

I hope you are able to take these ideas and lessons and put them into use to increase your own success. I also hope you are able to look at the world and the games you play in a new light. A light that will allow you to think outside of the box, or better yet, combine boxes in a way that can lead you to new levels of success you have never before dreamed.

Like any large-scale idea or vision the people that are a part of it matters greatly. For me these ideas are truly successful when they not only help you become better, but also empower you to help others become better as well. With over 30 years video game experience I don't see myself giving up video games anytime soon, so it is best that I make the most of the time spent.

The End Of The Journey Or New Game + ?

I want to be able to share the lessons I've learned in a fun and engaging way that is more understandable or at least more interesting than how I learned them. I want to inspire others to challenge themselves and find a way to take what they have learned in their hobby and feel the excitement of that same breakthrough in the workplace.

I want you to have epic wins in your 9-to-5, not just from 5 to 9 (shout out to Nick Loper of *Side Hustle Nation*). It is also my hope that someday, developers will find a way to create fun and engaging games that can also teach meaningful, high-level skills and challenge the thought process of how we approach the entertainment medium that is the video game.

I believe the key to a good educational game will be built upon a fun, engaging game that hides underneath it principles, concepts, and lessons that can be explored fully using all the advantages that video games have to offer, simultaneously overcoming many of the limitations we find in the workplace and educational system today.

In other words, don't settle for just being a hero in a video game. Be a hero in real life.

"Everybody loves a hero. Everybody loves you."

Viewtiful Joe

EPILOGUE

All the flowers in the field of hours

Have withered away

And the sky that used to light our lives

Is ashen grey

As the clouds kiss the faultline

  And look back as if to say…

  "There's nothing to see here…"

"There's nothing to feel here"

  And our dreams left like children by the wayside…

Seaside, by the Echoing Green

Why Did You Give Up?

Have you ever been pursuing a dream or a passion, only to have someone shoot it down?

It can be crushing to give up on a dream. Fear can take many forms. We all have different reasons for why we might call it quits, but the worst reason is giving up because of what others might think. So what if they

263

don't like what you have to say – you may lose a fan, but you'll keep your dream.

Be relentless. Like *Space Invaders*.

Back in college I had short lived dreams of being a graphic artist. Drawing used to be my number one hobby. Growing up, every time my family went for a ride in the car, I would take along a clipboard with blank sheets of paper and my set of pencils. In the afternoons when my family took their daily nap, I would stay up drawing. In the evening while the family gathered in the living room, I would be drawing, often ignoring the TV just to finish up a sketch.

In high school, I spent almost as much time drawing, and maybe even more time once I discovered Photoshop on the computer. I even placed 1st in the state during my Junior year in the FACCS competition, in the category of Digital Media. While in college, I took a part time job as a graphic artist with a local startup company – but it did not look like I hoped it would. Suddenly my hobby became a hassle. I spent most of my time undoing my vision for a particular project, and redoing things to match my bosses' ideas. The final product was not as dynamic or as interesting as where I tried to take things. When I would get home, I just felt so discouraged that drawing was the last thing I wanted to do.

So I gave up.

I let the resistance win. So ended my career in the digital arts.

But it does not have to stop there. Don't let other people's opinions keep you from pursuing your passions, or even making a career out of them. While we may regret some things that we do, more often we regret things that we wanted to do but did not.

Don't live a life wondering what might have been – get clear on what matters most, focus relentlessly on this and get moving!

For more on the "resistance" and overcoming it, check out Steven Pressfield's *The War of Art*.

BONUS CHAPTER

As a special bonus I wanted to include a series of lessons from a live action web-series based on the *Street Fighter* franchise. I included this in the book, as I believe the takeaways were important and the messaging provides a summary of many important lessons that we can learn from video games and the gaming industry. I also whole heartedly recommend picking up the Blu Ray or DVD of the series, you will not be disappointed.

8 Life & Leadership Lessons From Street Fighter: Assassin's Fist

Thanks to the amazing cast & crew of *Street Fighter: Assassin's Fist* (SF:AF), fans of the game have a live action series with an amazingly well written story, compelling acting, faithful and respectful treatment of the source material with top notch fight choreography, that successfully adds depth and maturity to the legacy of the series. Best of all, it feels like *Street Fighter*.

In the spirit of allegamy, I present to you 8 life and leadership lessons that can be seen in *Street Fighter: Assassin's Fist*.

To Go Further, You Need A Sparring Partner

In the chapter about Teamwork & Collaboration in this book, I wrote about the value that having a rival peer can bring to your success. In SF:AF we see how first, Goki & Goken, and then, Ryu & Ken are able to bring out their very best by having each other as a rivals. The desire to win, challenged by the competence and strength of another equal, or near equal, pushed all these martial artists to go further than if they had just been training on their own.

Shortcuts To Greatness Come With A Price

The four main characters in this story (and Gotetsu before them) are all subject to the temptation of taking a shortcut to mastering the ways of Ansatsuken, by tapping in to dark *Hado* - or *Satsui no Hado*. While this technique allows them to quickly channel immense power, the effects on the practitioner are dangerous, if not soul jeopardizing.

In life, it can be tempting to take shortcuts through questionable means, and many individuals have been consumed or disgraced by it. Sure you can make good money selling stolen goods or by dealing drugs, but at what cost to you personally? Even if you are successful, who you are may be destroyed in the process, just as Goki is transformed into

Akuma. While Akuma may be a powerful character to play in the game series, he leads a solitary and tortured life, fueled by hatred, envy, unfulfilled ambition, and his soul is restless and consumed by evil.

Thanks, I'll pass.

Success Only Has Meaning When You Have Others To Share It With

Ken's father (Mr. Masters) finds this out the hard way. After the death of Ken's mother, Mr. Masters leaves his son with Gouken to pursue his career (as well as help install discipline into Ken, who has been getting into trouble). Absent from Ken's life for many years, Mr. Masters successfully establishes his business, only to realize that it is no good if you don't have anyone to share it with. He returns to find Ken a grown man, with the hopes that he will return to work in the family business.

Ken's father begins to re-establish the relationship with his son, even providing him and Ryu with some training in boxing (a sport that he has since returned to practicing). There was something really emotional about the scene where Ken and his father are training together – you can see the relationship healing as the two of them are finally able to bond.

The same holds true for all of us. What good is it to achieve success, if there is no one around to enjoy the success with us? Keep your loved ones close and make them part of your success journey.

Don't Give Up

When you are just about to quit, you may be on the verge of a breakthrough. In the first episode of the series, Ken is ready to resign. After years of training and hard work, Ken and Ryu still have not learned the advanced techniques of *Hado*.

Feeling that Sensei Gouken is not sharing the secrets of Ansatsuken, Ken is prepared to leave the dojo and move on with his life. Ken approaches Gouken to inform him that he is leaving, but Ryu intervenes and declares that he and Ken are ready for the next level of training. Finally, Gouken agrees to teach his students the secrets of *Hado*.

If Ken had called it quits at that moment, he would have missed the life changing training that shaped his future. How often are we ready to give up or quit, without realizing how close we are to success?

When you reach the moment when you feel like you cannot go on, that might be a sign that you are just about to have the breakthrough you have been waiting for… stick with it.

Remember To Have Fun Along The Way

Sometimes we can get too caught up in the goal and focus of what we are doing, we can forget that what we do is not who we are. The best way to stay connected with this idea, is set aside time for fun, hobbies that may look nothing like what we do for work. In episode 10 of SF:AF we get to see Ryu and Ken unwinding by playing *Mega Man 2* (one of my all time favorite games).

The Ends Do Not Always Justify The Means

Some approaches may be illegal, immortal, or just unwise. The last of those three is the most difficult to deal with. Just because something is legal does not mean it is a good idea – there is a great cost to pay when using a dangerous force, as Goki finds out.

Results Come From Focus

When Goki is free of the distraction of the dojo and the expectations of others, he becomes completely focused on channeling dark *Hado*. He is then able to tap into even more powerful versions of the techniques of *Ansatsuken*. The result is the *Mestu hadoken*, capable of destroying a rock wall.

I cannot over emphasize the importance of focus to being effectively productive in our own lives. The power of focus can be further enhanced to enter a state of productivity 'flow' where time seems to disappear, and results and creativity seem to appear without resistance. Time management guru (and Karate Black Belt) David Allen says this about focus:

> *"Putting your mind to something (focus) activates both the subject and the object of your thinking. The body neurologically begins to respond as if the thought is true, and ideas start living a life of their own. Thoughts can occur a second time much easier than the first. Merely having thoughts is one thing. Consciously feeding them is quite another. You are powerful all the time, by way of your attention and intention. The question is, toward what are you pointing that power?"*

Know Your Own Unique Strengths

Gouken offers words of advice to both Ken and Ryu to prepare them for their upcoming battle against each other. The wisdom he shares is unique to each person: he speaks to Ryu in Japanese, telling him to not hold back in the match. Gouken addresses Ken in English, telling him to use aggression and focus to overwhelm his opponent.

Success looks different for each of us. Just like Ryu describes his flow of ki as cool and powerful, Ken identifies a fire flowing through him. What works for other people, may not work the same way for you. This is the importance of being authentic to who you are.

Too often, I have seen businesses try to apply a "best practice" expecting the same result in the company that some other organization was able to achieve. Using the same methods does not guarantee the same results. Ryu and Ken both practiced the same martial art, under the direction of the same teacher, but once they established the essential core of their discipline, their styles began reflect their unique character.

Trying to be someone else will not lead to success any more than ignoring the proven fundamentals of any effort will.

NOTES

Introduction

Dignan, A. (2011). Game frame: Using games as a strategy for success. Free Press. New York, NY.

The Entertainment Software Association. (2014. Essential Facts About the Computer And Video Game Industry.

Pressing Start

Harrison, J. (2014) 'Aesop for a digital age' The Computer Games Journal 3(2b) (Special Edition - 'What is missing from games?'), pp.196 - 199.

McGonigal, J. (2011). Reality is broken: Why games make us better and how they can change the world. New York: Penguin Press.

Rosser, J. (2008). Playin' to win: A surgeon, scientist and parent examines the upside of video games. Garden City, NY: Morgan James Publishing, LLC.

Dota 2 - The International - Overview. (n.d.). Retrieved January 2, 2015, from http://www.dota2.com/international/overview/

University Turns To E-Sports For New Scholarship Opportunities. (n.d.). Retrieved December 10, 2014, from http://www.npr.org/2014/11/17/364760854/university-turns-to-e-sports-for-new-scholarship-opportunities

Wingfield, N. (2014, December 8). E-Sports at College, With Stars and Scholarships. Retrieved December 10, 2014, from http://www.nytimes.com/2014/12/09/technology/esports-colleges-breeding-grounds-professional-gaming.html

Allegamy In Practice

7Bit Hero. (2014, March 16). Bubble Dragon: A Bubble Bobble Tribute. Retrieved March 18, 2014, from https://www.youtube.com/watch?v=WTL4V4GhKi4

Harrison, J. (2014, October 10). ClassicallyTrained Podcast Episode 10 - Interview with Hans Van Vliet of 7Bit Hero. Retrieved October 10, 2014, from http://classicallytrained.net/10/

Chrono Compendium. (n.d.). Retrieved November 2, 2014, from http://www.chronocompendium.com/Term/Chrono_Testament.html

Game Theory: Chrono Trigger Retells the BIBLE?!? (2013, August 8). Retrieved October 14, 2014, from https://www.youtube.com/watch?v=x-Sp62q2FAY

Campbell, J. (1972). The hero with a thousand faces (2d ed.). Princeton, N.J.: Princeton University Press.

GameChurch - Patrick Stafford and the State of Christian Video Games. (2014, August 29). Retrieved August 29, 2014, from https://itunes.apple.com/us/podcast/gamechurch/id900630285?mt=2

Netherlands Organization for Scientific Research (2009, May 27). Half of your friends lost in seven years, social network study finds. ScienceDaily. ScienceDaily, 27 May 2009.

Journey Collector's Edition. (2012, August 28). Developers Commentary. Thatgamecompany.

Lewis, C. (1956). Surprised by joy: The shape of my early life. New York: Harcourt, Brace.

Game Designer Kellee Santiago Responds to Roger Ebert's "Video Games Are Not Art" Rant. (2010, April 20). Retrieved October 2, 2014, from http://www.fastcompany.com/1621426/game-designer-kellee-santiago-responds-roger-eberts-video-games-are-not-art-rant

Tidball, J. (2010, February 18). Allegory In Video Games. Retrieved November 13, 2014, from http://gameplaywright.net/2010/02/allegory-in-video-games/

Not Quite Gamification

Zichermann, G., & Cunningham, C. (2011). Gamification by design: Implementing game mechanics in web and mobile apps. Sebastopol, Calif.: O'Reilly Media.

Pink, D. (2009). Drive: The surprising truth about what motivates us. New York, NY: Riverhead Books.

Csikszentmihalyi, M. (1990). Flow: The psychology of optimal experience. New York: Harper & Row.

The New Playlist For More Productive Work: Video Game Soundtracks. (2014, May 14). Retrieved January 2, 2015, from http://www.fastcompany.com/3030502/agendas/the-new-playlist-for-more-productive-work-video-game-soundtracks

The Rule of 52 and 17: It's Random, But it Ups Your Productivity. (2014). Retrieved from https://www.themuse.com/advice/the-rule-of-52-and-17-its-random-but-it-ups-your-productivity

Connecting The Dots

Harrison, J. (2014, August 22). ClassicallyTrained Podcast Episode 3: Interview with Simon Sinek. Retrieved August 22, 2014, from http://classicallytrained.net/podcast-interview-with-simon-sinek/

Merriam-Webster - Principle. (n.d.). Retrieved November 2, 2014, from http://www.merriam-webster.com/dictionary/principle

Zigarmi, D., Zigarmi, P., & Essary, V. (2014). What Do We Know About Development Level? 2014 The Ken Blanchard Companies.

Gladwell, M., & Rea, B. (2011). Malcolm Gladwell collected: The definitive editions. New York City: Little, Brown and Company.

Johnson, S. (2005). Everything bad is good for you: How today's popular culture is actually making us smarter. New York: Riverhead Books.

Gee, J. (2003). What video games have to teach us about learning and literacy. New York: Palgrave Macmillan.

Kotter, J., & Rathgeber, H. (2006). Our iceberg is melting: Changing and succeeding under any conditions. New York: St. Martin's Press.

Kotter, J. (1996). Leading change. Boston, Mass.: Harvard Business School Press.

Hyatt, M. (2013). The 10 Biggest Mistakes People Make in Setting Goals. Retrieved October 2, 2014, from http://michaelhyatt.com/10-biggest-goalsetting-mistakes.html

Adaptability

Ellis, A., & Lange, A. (1994). How to keep people from pushing your buttons. New York N.Y.: Carol Pub.

Musk, E. (2014, June 12). All Our Patent Are Belong To You. Retrieved June 12, 2014, from http://www.teslamotors.com/blog/all-our-patent-are-belong-you

Patterson, K. (2002). Crucial conversations: Tools for talking when stakes are high. New York: McGraw-Hill.

Covey, S. (1989). The seven habits of highly effective people: Restoring the character ethic. New York: Simon and Schuster.

Change Management

Kotter, J., & Rathgeber, H. (2006). Our iceberg is melting: Changing and succeeding under any conditions. New York: St. Martin's Press.

Kotter, J. (1996). Leading change. Boston, Mass.: Harvard Business School Press.

Heath, C., & Heath, D. (2010). Switch: How to change things when change is hard. New York: Broadway Books.

Flynn, P. (2014, February 18). How I Increased my Email Subscriptions by 315% (And the Small, Quick Thing That Made it Happen). Retrieved October 2, 2014, from http://www.smartpassiveincome.com/quick-wins/

Pascale, R., & Sternin, J. (2010). The power of positive deviance: How unlikely innovators solve the world's toughest problems. Boston, Mass.: Harvard Business Press.

Clearing The Entitlement Stage

Maslow, A.H. (1943). "A Theory of Human Motivation". In Psychological Review, 50 (4), 430-437. Washington, DC: American Psychological Association.

Andrews, A. (2013, July 20). Podcast Episode 94: How To Practice Gratitude.

Easley, J., & Harrison, J. (2014, February 8). Starve The Doubts Episode 70: Dr. Marshall Goldsmith - Is it Worth it? http://www.starvethedoubts.com/70-dr-marshall-goldsmith-is-it-worth-it/

Personal Accountability

Harrison, J. (2014, September 11). ClassicallyTrained Podcast Episode 06 - Interview with David Hayter. http://classicallytrained.net/06

Lencioni, P. (2012). The Advantage: Why organizational health trumps everything else in business. San Francisco, CA. Jossey-Bass.

Miller, J. (2004). QBQ! The Question Behind the Question: Practicing Personal Accountability at Work and in Life. New York, NY: The Penguin Group.

Glanz, B. (1996). Care Packages for the Workplace: Dozens of Little Things You Can Do To Regenerate Spirit At Work. New York, NY: McGraw-Hill.

Innovation

Brogan, C. (2014). The Freaks Shall Inherit the Earth: Entrepreneurship for Weirdos, Misfits, and World Dominators. Hoboken, New Jersey: John Wiley & Sons.

Strengths

Buckingham, M., & Clifton, D. (2001). Now, Discover Your Strengths. New York, NY: The Free Press.

Rath, T. (2007). StrengthsFinder 2.0. New York, NY: Gallup Press.

Buckingham, M. (2010). Go Put Your Strengths to Work: 6 Powerful Steps to Achieve Outstanding Performance. New York, NY: Free Press.

Harrison, J. (2014, January 20). Life Changers: John Saddington – You Don't Have to be Good at Everything. Retrieved from http://jondharrison.com/2014/01/20/life-changers-john-saddington/

Learning

Blanchard, K., & Peale, N. (1988). The Power of Ethical Management. New York, NY: William Morrow and Company.

Skorka-Brown, J., Andrade, J. & May, J. (2014). 'Playing 'Tetris' reduces the strength, frequency and vividness of naturally occurring cravings' Appetite 76, 161-16.

Holmes, E., James, E., Kilford, E., & Deeprose, C. (2010). Key steps in developing a cognitive vaccine against traumatic flashbacks: visuospatial Tetris versus verbal Pub Quiz. PLoS ONE, 5(11), e13706.

Haier, R., Karama, S., Leyba, L., & Jung, R. (2009). MRI assessment of cortical thickness and functional activity changes in adolescent girls following three months of practice on a visual-spatial task. BMC Research Notes 2009, 2:174.

Sanbonmatsu, D., Strayer, D., Medeiros-Ward, N., Watson, J. (2013). Who Multi-Tasks and Why? Multi-Tasking Ability, Perceived Multi-Tasking Ability, Impulsivity, and Sensation Seeking. PLoS ONE 8(1): e54402.

Allen, D. (2002). Getting Things Done: The Art of Stress-Free Productivity. New York, NY: The Penguin Group.

Harrison, J. (2013, October 7). Life Changers: David Allen - Stress Free Productivity. Retrieved from http://jondharrison.com/2013/10/07/life-changers-david-allen-stress-free-productivity/

Communication & Learning

Mehrabian, A. (1972). Silent Messages: Implicit Communication of Emotions and Attitudes. Belmont, CA: Wadsworth Publishing Company.

Covey, S. (1989). The seven habits of highly effective people: Restoring the character ethic. New York: Simon and Schuster.

Thompson, G., & Jenkins, J. (2013). Verbal Judo: The Gentle Art of Persuasion, Updated Edition. New York, NY: HarperCollins.

Chart Moves: 'Halo 4' Sets Record as Highest-Charting Video Game Soundtrack Ever. (2012, November 1). Retrieved from http://www.billboard.com/biz/articles/news/1083194/chart-moves-halo-4-sets-record-as-highest-charting-video-game-soundtrack.

Teamwork & Collaboration

Godin, S. (2002). Survival Is Not Enough: Zooming, Evolution, and the Future of Your Company. New York, NY: Free Press.

Belbin, R. (1993). Team roles at work. Oxford: Butterworth-Heinemann.

Knowledge Sharing

Nikravan, L. (2011). Why Communication From Leadership is Essential For Success. Chief Learning Officer Magazine. Chicago, IL: MediaTec Publishing, Inc.

Merchant, N. (2014). The New How: Creating Business Solutions Through Collaborative Strategy. Sebastopol, CA: O'Reilly Media.

Stanley, A. (2013). Organizational Clarity. Chick-fil-a Leadercast. Atlanta, GA.

Sinek, S. (2009). Start with why: How great leaders inspire everyone to take action. New York: Portfolio.

Persistence & Grit

Duckworth, A. (2013). Angela Lee Duckworth: The Key To Success? Grit. [Video file]. Retrieved from http://www.ted.com/talks/angela_lee_duckworth_the_key_to_success_grit?language=en

Harrison, J. (2014). The Surprising Success Trait That Video Games Teach Us. Retrieved November 7, 2014, from http://goodmenproject.com/ethics-values/success-trait-video-games-already-teach-us/

How Celldweller's persistence paid off. (2013, June 24). Retrieved from http://www.themusicninja.com/tmn-resident-artist-interview-how-celldwellers-persistence-paid-off/

Tracy, B. (1988). Pathways Toward Personal Progress. The Effective Manager Seminar Series. Wheeling, IL: Nightingale Conant.

Brian Tracy is Chairman and CEO of Brian Tracy International, a company specializing in the training and development of individuals and organizations. Brian's goal is to help people achieve their personal and business goals faster and easier than they ever imagined.

Brian Tracy has consulted for more than 1,000 companies and addressed more than 5,000,000 people in 5,000 talks and seminars throughout the US, Canada and 55 other countries worldwide. As a Keynote speaker and seminar leader, he addresses more than 250,000 people each year.

For more information on Brian Tracy programs, go to: www.briantracy.com

Conclusion

Acuff, J. (2013). Start: Punch fear in the face, escape average, do work that matters. Brentwood, TN: Lampo Press.

Wells, E. (2014, October 15). EP56: How to Merge Your Passions for a Happy Life w/ Jon D. Harrison. Retrieved from http://www.ellorywells.com/ep56-jon-harrison-classically-trained/

Epilogue

Belville, J. (2004). Seaside. The Echoing Green. On The Winter of Our Discontent. Seattle, WA. BEC Recordings.

Bonus Chapter

Street Fighter: Assassin's Fist [Motion picture]. (2014). U.S.A.: Funimation.

ABOUT THE AUTHOR

Jon D. Harrison, MBA/HRM, ODCC is a Certified Organizational Development Consultant, author, speaker, blogger, and podcaster. His unique approach to teaching business, leadership, and life lessons with video game analogy and metaphor has appeared on FastCompany, Lifehacker, The Good Men Project, Monster, The NY Daily News, The Palm Beach Post, NG4, IGN, The Computer Games Journal, and more. His skills range from individual coaching to speaking to large audiences of several hundred.

Jon's personal Focus is helping others succeed through leveraging and teaching problem solving approaches. He enjoys communicating and translating ideas to help others live a more effective life.

A retro game collector, his favorite systems in his collection include the Neo Geo AES, Nintendo Virtual Boy, NEC Turbo Express, Sega Dreamcast, Nintendo Entertainment System and Super Nintendo. He enjoys quirky games, as well as games that can make him laugh or cry. Usually laugh.

Jon is a Florida native where he resides with his wife and son.

About ClassicallyTrained

Blog

Jon D. Harrison writes about effective leadership and personal productivity solutions made accessible through video game metaphor and analogy, delivered in a fun, engaging, and professional manner at *ClassicallyTrained.net*.

Each week, readers can also find motivational quotes from their favorite video games.

Podcast

A weekly podcast featuring content similar to the writing found on ClassicallyTrained.net as well as interviews with business leaders, bestselling authors, voice actors, and other influential members of the video game industry.

Available in iTunes & Sticher.

GAMES MENTIONED

Introduction

Final Fantasy X
Parasite Eve II
World Of Warcraft
Doom
Halo

Pressing Start

Half Life 2
Reader Rabbit
Mathblaster
Kingdom Hearts
Final Fantasy VII
League of Legends
Defender of the Ancients 2

Allegamy In Practice

The Prince of Persia: The Sands of Time
Bubble Bobble
Chrono Trigger
Final Fantasy
Dragon Quest

Not Quite Gamification

Parappa The Rapper
Super Mario World

Connecting The Dots

The World Ends With You
The Legend of Zelda
Rival Schools
Power Stone
Battletoads
Final Fantasy XIII-2

Strategic Planning

Call of Duty: Advanced Warfare
Super Mario Bros. 3
NBA Jam
TMNT: Tournament Fighters
Clayfighter
Final Fantasy Tactics
Command and Conquer
Starcraft
Dark Souls
Resident Evil 4

Adaptability

Bioshock
Tekken
Tekken 3
Dead or Alive
Marvel vs Capcom
King of the Fighters
Zero Wing
Missile Command

Final Fantasy VIII
The Legend of Zelda

Change Management

Katamari Forever
Katamari Damacy
Me and My Katamari
We Love Katamari
Re: Mission
Re: Mission 2
Mega Man 2

Clearing The Entitlement Level

Final Fantasy VII
The Legend of the Dragoon
Castlevania: Symphony of the Night
Noby Noby Boy
Katamari Damacy
Tekken
Galaga
Sonic the Hedgehog
Animal Crossing
Kirby's Dreamland

Personal Accountability

Animal Crossing: New Leaf
Metal Gear Solid
Oddworld: Abe's Odessy
Ninja Gaiden
Strider

Teenage Mutant Ninja Turtles
Double Dragon
Bionic Commando
Resident Evil
Mega Man 2

Innovation

Final Fantasy XIII
Tempest
Pac Man
Tempest 2000
Space Invaders
Alien vs Preadator
Rayman
Silent Hill
Final Fantasy VII
Final Fantasy VII: Crisis Core

Strengths

Devil May Cry 2
Street Fighter 2
Mortal Kombat
Killer Instinct
Street Fighter IV
Super Street Fighter IV

Learning

Max Payne 2
Tetris
Angry Birds

Candy Crush

Communication & Listening

Zero Wing
Metal Gear
Final Fantasy VII
Pro Wrestling
Dodonpachi
Ghosts'n Goblins
Samurai Shodown 2
Metal Gear Solid
Metal Gear Solid 4
Asteroids
Combat
Mega Man 2
Castlevania: Symphony of the Night
Suikoden
Castlevania: Bloodlines
Contra: Hard Corps
Final Fantasy VI

Teamwork & Collaboration

Maniac Mansion
M.U.L.E.
Metal Slug
Gunstar Heroes
X Men Arcade
Knights of the Round
Contra
Streets Of Rage
Gauntlet

Smash TV
Battletoads
Final Fight
Street Fighter II
Mortal Kombat
Virtua Fighter
Tekken
Killer Instinct
Samurai Shodown
Final Fight 2
Streets Of Rage 3
Super Street Fighter II
Killer Instinct 2
Mortal Kombat 2
Super Mario Kart
GoldenEye 007
1943
Galaga
Super Mario Bro.s
Double Dragon
Mega Man
Sonic The Hedgehog 2
Rocket Knight Adventures
Suikoden
Final Fantasy VI

Knowledge Sharing

Metal Gear Solid 2: Sons of Liberty
Pong
Tetris
Final Fantasy XIII
Castlevania 2: Simon's Quest

Faxanadu
Double Dragon

Persistence & Grit

Phantasy Star 2
Castlevania III: Dracula's Curse
Top Gun
Yo! Noid
Ghosts'n Goblins
The Silver Surfer
Double Dragon III: The Sacred Stones
Assassin's Creed 2
Dead Rising 2
The Need for Speed: Most Wanted
Joust

Conclusion

Final Fantasy X
Perfect Dark
Bomberman 64
Street Fighter IV
Galaga
Joust
Tetris
That Dragon, Cancer
Grand Theft Auto V
Call of Duty: Advanced Warfare
To The Moon
Flower
Journey
Viewtiful Joe

Thank you for reading

www.ingramcontent.com/pod-product-compliance
Lightning Source LLC
Chambersburg PA
CBHW070850180526
45168CB00005B/1765